G000135951

THE MAKING OF THE
MIDDLE THAMES

The Making of

DAVID GORDON WILSON

the Middle Thames

SPURBOOKS LIMITED

Published by Spurbooks Limited
6 Parade Court, Bourne End, Buckinghamshire

© David Gordon Wilson 1977

All Rights Reserved:
No part of this publication may be
reproduced, stored in a retrieval system,
or transmitted in any form or by any means,
electronic, photocopying, recording or otherwise,
without the permission of the publisher.

ISBN 0 904978 23 0

Designed and Produced by
Mechanick Exercises, London

Typesetting by Inforum, Portsmouth

Printed in Great Britain by
Chapel River Press, Andover, Hants

Bound by Mansell, Witham, Essex

CONTENTS

ILLUSTRATIONS

ACKNOWLEDGEMENTS

My grateful thanks to the following organisations and individuals for allowing me to use material and for supplying information without which this book could not have been written.

The Buckinghamshire Archaeological Society for research facilities and material from the "Records of Bucks" and the Court Rolls of Hedsor Manor. The Berkshire Archaeological Society for quotations from the Berkshire Archeological Journal. Mr. J.C. Badcock for allowing me to examine the papers of Lord Boston of Hedsor and Mr. T.G.F.B. Irby for permission to quote from them. Illustrations from "Life on the Upper Thames" courtesy of Virtue and Company. Christopher Stanley, Luke Over and Ray Weng for archaeological information prior to publication. The Thames Conservancy Division of the Thames Water Authority, Maidenhead Library, Ray Weng and Messrs Salters for prints and photographs. Christopher Stanley for aerial photographs. Mr. E.M. Hazelton for plans of Marlow and Miss E.A. Upson, Mrs. V. Johansen, Miss R. Jackson, Mr. L.F. Lunnon and Mr. A. Spindler for photographs from family collections. The librarians and library staff at Maidenhead and Marlow for their patience and excellent service over a number of years. John Williams and Jim Franklin for photographic printing. Transcripts of Crown Copyright records in the Public Record Office and Buckinghamshire Record Office appear by permission of the Controller of H.M. Stationery Office.

12

INTRODUCTION

On hearing the Thames referred to as 'liquid history', most people probably conjure up images of the great pageants of the past on the river at London, and other colourful historic events at Runnymede, Hampton Court and Windsor; but to me the term implies a less obtrusive but far more fascinating history — the story of human activity throughout many centuries, moulding the river into what it is today, a story which began deep in the mists of prehistory. The history and topography of one comparatively small area of the Middle Thames illustrates the taming of a natural river valley from the time of the first riverside settlements of stone-age man up to the present day sites of towns and villages, fisheries, mills and weirs, which were already well established when Danish long-ships sailed up the estuary.

The way of life of the people of the valley was little different from that of the rest of their countrymen living throughout the lowlands. However, I have concentrated my efforts on piecing together the evidence of thousands of years of human occupation and river navigation in the area in which I was born and spent my childhood, and in which I still live and work. Reliable up-to-date archaeological reports and previously unpublished documents from the area encompassing Bray, Maidenhead, Cookham and Marlow have been used to trace in detail the pattern of settlement, the development of the road system, the working life of the people of the land, and their reliance on the river which provided natural resources of food, materials and power.

From the earliest times the river provided man with a natural highway from the sea into the heart of England. The growth of commercial navigation of the Thames and its connecting waterways is outlined from local and national aspects with particular attention to the construction and navigation of various types of 'Westerne Barges' which for a thousand years traded up and down the length of the river. Many rivermen remember with regret the last days of com-

Bray-on-Thames

mercial navigation and I am grateful for their help in providing some details to bring that chapter to its final close.

As the barge traffic declined, people began to use the river increasingly for leisure activities and throughout the almost legendary Victorian period and up until today, the pleasure boating industry has flourished. The Thames Valley has become one of the great tourist centres of Britain and each year thousands enjoy a boating holiday on the river. There are also vast numbers of private boat owners who flock to the boat-yards every summer weekend for a well earned break from the world of commerce and industry.

Today as never before, we are dependent on the river for the disposal of waste products and the supply of vital fresh water and the authorities are placing ever increasing emphasis on water conservation. At the same time there is an increasing awareness that the wild life, flowers and trees, all contribute to the health and beauty of the countryside, enriching our lives, and must therefore be protected.

My apparent passion for the river and the people of the past arises from my work and travels on the river and from a long-standing interest in archaeology and local history. Many published works have been consulted in search of material and I bear a debt of gratitude to past researchers. The investigation has been long and sometimes tedious for one can read fifty books on the Thames and find little that applies to the river itself. Most of the old histories dealt mainly with the riverside mansions of the elite and were not about the ordinary people; farmers, fishermen, millers, lock builders and bargemen, who lived and died working in the valley, who knew it in all its moods, from summer drought to winter flood, and who made it what it is today.

The grandeur of the great loop of the Middle Thames from Maidenhead to Marlow is scarcely surpassed anywhere on the river. Situated halfway between London and Oxford and forming the boundary between the rich agricultural counties of Berkshire and Buckinghamshire, it has always been one of the busiest stretches, and in more recent times one of the most popular and fashionable. To set the scene let us embark on a short journey and note the items of interest as they appear.

As one cruises upstream from Bray to Maidenhead, the first attractions are the huge dark red brick spans of Brunel's famous railway bridge, closely followed by the arches of Maidenhead's historic

Boulters Lock with Ray Mill Stream and the weir stream

Winter Hill and Spade Oak Reach

bridge, set on the line of the old Great West Road. Just beyond lies
Skindles Hotel, followed by other scattered remnants of the town's
once elegant Victorian and Edwardian past. Then comes the dark
chasm of Boulter's Lock, one of the largest on the river, and the most
popular, invariably hemmed in by a wall of sightseers during
weekends in summer.

As the last great Victorian mansion is left behind, the renowned
Cliveden Reach opens up ahead. To the left there are gentle meadows typical of the floodplain, and to the right, for a distance of two
miles from Taplow to Hedsor, a massed array of countless varieties
of trees clinging to the almost vertical face of the chalk cliff of Cliveden, crowned at its highest point by the stately mansion, now
owned by the National Trust.

At the top of the reach we approach the beautiful Hedsor bend, at
the mouth of the valley of the Buckinghamshire Wye. Here in the centre of several ancient channels lies Cookham Lock, in the most beautiful and secluded setting on the river. Next comes the long lockcut,
said to be one of the most attractive of the artificial cuttings, turning
westward and opening out into the brightness of the broad Cookham Reach, and presenting a view of the bridge and the ancient
church, behind which lies picturesque Cookham Village, of Saxon
origins. A pleasant variety of riverside houses now appears on the
right and to the left stretches the second National Trust property on
this short trip, the lush expanse of Cockmarsh, sharply terminating
to the south in the gentle slope of Rowborough Hill.

Proceeding beyond Bourne End, the floodplain opens out to the

16

Marlow Bridge

right, in the distance gradually rising into the upward slope of a series of great gravel terraces, capped by thick woods. On the floodplain, a short way from the river is Little Marlow, another ancient village, completely unspoilt. To the left the green of Rowborough gradually rises to the heights of Cookham Dean, culminating in the well-known landmark of Winter Hill. The river is now bisected by tree-clad islands, the nesting haunt of duck, swan and grebe. At the islands the chalk escarpment hugs the river's edge and then further along gradually curves away, clad in the ever-changing colours of the beeches of Quarry Woods.

The river now takes a sharp turn to the right and Marlow appears, framed in the wide and graceful span of the new road bridge. Next comes Marlow Lock, surrounded by some interesting Georgian and Victorian architecture, and also some curious modern structures. Beyond lies the foaming curve of the weir, the Compleat Angler Hotel, and our final graceful feature, the Marlow suspension bridge, gateway to an attractive old town, full of buildings of character and as yet unspoilt by modern development.

1 · THE PEOPLE
OF THE VALLEY

The Chiltern Hills to the north form a backdrop to the river as it sweeps around the final bend of the Henley loop and under the chalk cliff of Taplow before embarking on rather less interesting meanders across the flatness of the London Basin. Contained within the Henley loop is the northern-most part of what was originally the Forest of Windsor and 'The Great Frithe' of which Maidenhead Thicket is a remnant. Ashley Hill and the chalk outliers of Remenham and Winter Hill dominate the area. Other geological features are the ancient Thames terraces which are particularly well defined at Maidenhead and Taplow.

Within the most north-easterly part of the loop lie the lands of the ancient Royal Manor of Cookham, still managing to retain an attractive village, extensive commons and pleasant farmlands. At one time Cookham was of economic importance to the Castle at Windsor and to the Crown, and still gives the impression of affluence often lacking in villages of a comparative size. Its former importance has left us some interesting administrative documents which give some idea of the way of life of ordinary country people during the Middle Ages. In fact the way of life of the English peasant, his farming techniques, living conditions and reliance on the community, changed little from the first Saxon settlement until the 19th century.

The Ice Age began around two million years ago and continued until about 12,000 B.C. There were four major periods when ice advanced to a variable extent across major portions of the earth. Each cold period was followed by an 'Interglacial' period in which the average temperatures increased, and climatic conditions in Europe improved from Arctic to temperate, even semi-tropical. During glacial conditions much of the landscape of the British Isles was moulded into its present contours by the erosive action of cold and ice. Surface rocks were reduced to boulders, gravel and mud by frost action, hills were carved into shape by glaciers of over one hundred feet in thickness. The resultant debris was ground down, sifted and graded, and indiscriminately dumped on hill and valley. On two occasions the Scandinavian ice sheet advanced as far south as the Chiltern Hills, bringing with it accumulated debris from as far afield as Norway.

As the ice melted, an early Thames channel was formed as a tributary of the Rhine, draining into the North Sea, and vast sheets of sands and gravels were deposited along the lower valley and estuary. Later, during the height of a warm interglacial period, the sea levels rose by several hundred feet or more and the waters of the Thames backed up and diminished in flow and scouring action. A floodplain was now formed. This acquired a capping of alluvium or 'brickearth' laid by periodic flooding. During the next glaciation the ice cap again took up a vast quantity of water causing the sea level to drop. The river now began a process of down-cutting through the floodplain until the thaw came again.

These actions were carried out on a vast scale. Early channels existed at four hundred feet above the present floodplain. Another is buried one hundred feet below the present estuary. Not only have sea levels changed from time to time, but there has also been an uplifting and tilting of the land. This tilt, together with the periodic build-up of the ice-cap north of the Chilterns, probably accounts for the gradual southerly drift of the successive Thames channels.

Deposition, downcutting and erosion have made the identification of the various terraces a very complicated process. However, the main terraces, which attain thicknesses of up to fifty feet, have been confirmed by geologists, and named after the locality in which they are most prominent in the middle Thames area. On parts of the southern slopes of the Chilterns, at heights of up to five hundred and fifty feet above sea level, there are high level marine deposits and pebble gravel. Below this, to the south there lies the Chiltern Drift and chalky boulder clay, deposited by ice. This in turn mixes with early river gravels and the so-called 'gravel trains', including the Winter Hill and Black Park terraces. These are contemporary with the second or main glaciation. Further down the slope, and running consecutively down to the present river, with outcrops on both sides of it, there are the Boyne Hill, Lynch Hill, Taplow and Upper and Lower floodplain terraces. Traces of other terraces and a buried channel have been identified on the upper river above Goring, but the most noticeable traces are those in the middle and lower Thames.

At some early time, possibly during or after the first glaciation, the enormous pressures of ice and dammed-up water forced a passage through the chalk escarpment to form the Goring Gap, after which the Thames ran south to join the Kennet at Reading, and then swung north and east through the Henley Loop to Marlow, Beaconsfield, and St. Albans, towards the east coast and the Wash. This early channel, which was several hundred feet above the present river, has left sand and gravel traces at places such as Winter Hill at Cookham and Black Park to the north of Slough and also in the Henley Loop. At some time during the first interglacial or into the second glaciation, about half a million years ago, man made his first appearance in the valley. Primitive flint hand-axes of the Abbe Villian culture have been found in the Henley Loop at Winter Hill levels.

About a quarter of a million years ago during the second interglacial, the climate was such that the elephant and hippopotamus thrived in the Thames Valley. At other times the climate was more temperate and familiar trees, such as birch, pine and oak, clothed the countryside. By now a second inundation had formed the Boyne Hill terrace at a lower level and the river was being turned south by the chalk escarpment between Hedsor and Maidenhead. For hundreds of thousands of years during the latter part of the Ice Age, Palaeolithic man hunted along the shores of a much younger Thames. The river saw many botanical changes on its banks, from the sparse vegetation of the tundra during glaciation, to the lushness of semi-tropical forest in the interglacial periods.

The men of the old Stone Age are shadowy figures, ape-like and, we are apt to think, stupid. Nevertheless the species managed to adapt and survive through great changes in a hostile world for a length of time beyond our comprehension. For much of that time, man needed but a few varieties of roughly chipped and flaked flint tools to augment his cunning and his bare hands.

The most well known of these tools is the hand-axe, great numbers of which have been found in recent times in the gravels and brickearths of the Thames Valley. The Boyne Hill Terrace in particular has produced many groups of the well-known Acheulian type, at Maidenhead, Burnham, Yiewsley and Swanscombe in Kent. The large numbers of tools which have been found in close proximity to each other suggest that these were habitation sites, but more often the finds are of single specimens which lie in drift deposits which may have originated miles away. The Acheulian style of hand-axe lasted for many thousands of years, possibly through the third glaciation, as these implements are found in the lower Lynch Hill and Taplow Terraces. However, many of these finds may be contained in drift deposits from upper levels. By this time the course of the river would be roughly where it is today, but still at a higher level.

By now other cultures were appearing, bringing Clactonian and Levallois flake tools, and we come to the last glaciation, beginning about fifty thousand years ago, during which Homo-Sapiens seem to have replaced Neanderthal man. It is possible that the Taplow and floodplain terraces were deposited during the last glaciation but the evidence is much disputed. These last terraces contain the remains of creatures such as the reindeer, musk-ox and woolly rhinoceros, showing that, for a time at least, tundra-like conditions prevailed.

The Thames is a meandering river, cutting its way through its own floodplain. There is a natural tendency for a gradual downstream meandering course by the scouring action on the outside of each bend. At the same time there is a build-up of silt on the inside of the bends where the current is less rapid. This continuous process can be plainly seen on the upper reaches above Oxford, where the channel passes through thick deposits of soft alluvium. The effect is less pronounced on the hard compacted gravels of the middle and lower river and other natural barriers affect the course to a greater or lesser degree. The solid greensand rock bed at Clifton Hampden, the Goring Gap, and the well-known chalk escarpment at Cliveden Reach have all provided opposition, but the river has eventually cut through, and visible undercutting still continues at Cliveden.

Running water will always find the lowest and easiest course, therefore the river will almost always keep to one main channel. Islands may be formed in the channel by deposits of gravels and silt in back eddies caused by obstructions. They may also be formed on outcrops of chalk on the river bed or on a bar of gravel at the tail of a particularly fast stretch of water. Exceptional spates during wet periods, especially in wintertime, help to scour the riverbed and also build up the banks. The latter effect is caused by the deposit of a layer of rich silt, or alluvium, over the floodplain when the river rises above 'bank high' conditions. Deposition is heavy near the river bank and thins out away from the river. Because of this, in many areas the floodplain is higher adjacent to the banks than it is towards the outer edge. Thus, swampy areas may be formed perhaps hundreds of yards from the river, and usually parallel to it. Since early times these areas have been artificially drained by ditching in order to diminish flooding and improve land productivity. Many of the present small streams on the floodplains were formed in this way.

So it can be seen that the Thames Valley was never a vast swamp, dotted with innumerable islands, as early antiquaries would have us believe. One such gentleman was the Chairman of the Buckinghamshire Architectural and Archaeological Society, the

Venerable Archdeacon Bickersteth, D.D. On 28th July, 1870 the Society made an excursion on the Thames at Marlow and was addressed by this gentleman, who proceeded to make out a case for the source of the Thames being in Bucks, with certain rivulets around Aylesbury forming the Thame. The two names, Thames and Thame, being so alike, they must be the same river! He went on to expound the theory that in primitive times "the Thames, instead of being confined within narrow banks as now, spread its water over a wide district and formed large lagoons, dotted with small islands. . ."

About twelve thousand years ago, the semi-arctic conditions in Western Europe were gradually becoming less severe. At this time the present south-east coast of Britain was still joined to the Continent by a land bridge. New cultures began to appear in the Thames Valley, as Mesolithic man, an advanced race, was better adapted to fish and hunt the smaller species of game abundant in the riverside thickets. The Mesolithic tribes brought weapons and implements of wood and bone, but like their predecessors relied heavily on the native flint for cutting tools. Their techniques, however, were vastly superior. A great variety of beautiful little flake tools was made, including cutters, scrapers, and borers, as well as points for arrows and spears. For forest clearance, larger axe-heads were also manufactured with transverse cutting edges which could be easily retouched.

For several thousand years the Mesolithic tribes roamed the British Isles, during which time the English Channel was formed and the climate became warmer, allowing our familiar forest trees to clothe the land. We can now identify many different cultures of this Middle Stone Age Period by the different varieties of flint tools which were developed, and by the type of country chosen as habitat. For instance, in Yorkshire the classic site is Starr Carr, a lake settlement, built on brushwood platforms. In Surrey the chosen ground included the sandy open heathland around Farnham. However, the Thames watershed was probably for the most part populated by the so-called Maglemosians, the forest people. The hunting groups seem to have ignored the main river, but were in every tributary valley. They lived close to their food supply of fish, game, wild fruits and plants, and moved on as it became depleted in a particular area. Very rarely do we find structural remains of their camps or the different perishable artifacts they must have used, but in some areas, particularly on the Loddon and Kennet, many thousands of their flint tools and waste flakes litter the riversides.

Recent archaeological discoveries made by dedicated amateur

22

Mesolithic flint tools from the Maidenhead area

archaeologists in the Maidenhead/Bray area show that this region has seen considerable settlement at each period of Man's colonisation of Southern England. For instance, the Mesolithic Period is represented by a site of major importance at Braywick, on an insignificant stream which rises on the sandy uplands to the south of Maidenhead and enters the Thames at nearby Bray. On the floodplain at Bisham there lies a buried channel of the main river containing peat to a considerable depth, with waterlogged treetrunks and branches, the remains of a considerable forest. Recent finds of nearby Mesolithic material leads one to believe that this may be one of the first sites to be found adjacent to the main river, albeit on a silting up-side channel. Other sites are known, or at least suspected from the number of recent surface finds. Thus we are leading to a major revision of opinion regarding the density of occupation during the Middle Stone Age. The same applies to the next period.

About 3,000 B.C. new waves of settlers began to arrive from Europe. They still used flint and stone tools but brought pottery, quern stones and other trappings of a more settled agricultural economy which had first developed in the Middle East several millennia before. Until recently it was thought that in Southern England the vast majority of Neolithic farmers and herdsmen settled on the open chalk downlands leaving their mark in the form of burial mounds and other large earthworks. Aerial photography now shows us that Neolithic settlement was just as extensive on the upper Thames gravels. It is likely that much of the virgin forest was cleared at this time, never to be re-established, and small fields of corn and cattle enclosures dotted the easily worked floodplain sands and gravels.

The same must apply to the Middle and Lower Thames, although up to now photography has been less revealing. However, one Thames-side site which deserves mention is Yeoveney Lodge Farm, Staines, which proved to be a huge causewayed camp of the early 'Windmill Hill' type of the Downlands. Extensive excavations were carried out by the Ministry of Works, but unfortunately no report has been issued.

During late Mesolithic times the sea was about ten metres below present levels and gradually rising. Therefore, even in the Neolithic period the river was also running at a lower level with the addition of same braided channels which have since silted up, as at Bisham. Another has been discovered at Bray, to the west of Queens Eyot, where gravel extraction following excavation by a local society has

24

The Antler Comb from Bray

exposed an extensive archaeological treasure-house on the floodplain terrace, proving that from the Neolithic period onwards this was thought to be a very agreeable place in which to settle. The Neolithic occupation layer was found about 40 cm. below the present height of the water table, immediately on top of an ancient gravel bank. The layer was rich in Neolithic pottery, flint tools, antler picks and one of the finest antler combs to be found in this country. Further Neolithic pottery is coming to light at nearby Braywick, some of which has fine decoration of a style which paradoxically can only be paralleled to material from the Orkney Isles!

From about 2,000 B.C. the Bray settlement experienced successive invasions from the Continent as waves of warlike Bronze-age peoples came sweeping up from the coast. The plodding locals were enslaved or cast out and a new village of wicker-work huts rose on the ruins of the first. As the river levels rose through the centuries, the huts had to be set on piles and dug-out canoes were used to get about. The village was always well guarded with an armoury of shining bronze swords, axes, spears and bows and flint-tipped arrows, for newcomers were often likely to appear round the bend of the river, and one never knew how uncivilized some of the foreigners might be. Many were the waterborn battles which left a litter of magnificent weapons on the river bed. The total number found in this area makes up one of the largest concentrations in Wessex.

Along the Thames Valley, stockaded villages of round huts became numerous, as did round burial mounds such as survive on the floodplain at Cookham. There were great religious and social centres, the so-called henge monuments, rivalling Stonehenge and Avebury but now buried beneath centuries of ploughing and inundation. The Thames was now an important trading highway, regularly used by large canoes and skin covered curraghs, even by Mediterranean vessels. As well as copper and bronze, there was traffic in tin, gold, amber and fine stone axes and other commodities which were traded to and from the Continent and even as far as Egypt and the Baltic.

About 600 B.C. expensive iron tools and weapons began to filter into England in the hands of new settlers whose culture has been named after its possible source, Hallstatt in Austria. It was not long before the old bronze-using peoples were swept away or subjugated by the technological superiority of the new invaders. Gradually the country was split into a succession of tribal states, overlorded by an aristocratic elite with strongholds at strategic points on hills or promontories, the well-known hillforts which still dominate the countryside today. There are a number on the hills overlooking the Thames Valley. Two which may have played a significant part in the area lie very close together at Medmenham. The one at Danesfield in particular has a spectacular position on the edge of a chalk cliff which rises vertically from the riverside.

Up to then, cultivation in the Thames Valley had been largely restricted to the poorer but more easily worked sands and gravels but now iron-shod implements allowed further forest clearance and ploughing on the heavier soils of the hill tops and slopes. Isolated groups of early iron age pottery have been found in unlikely places in the Maidenhead area and of course elsewhere, the only remaining evidence of isolated farmsteads where a hard-working family once eked out a bare existence. However, we must again look to the riverside gravels for the main farmlands and there is no doubt that the clearances of previous settlers were fully utilized. Land which is over-cropped soon becomes exhausted and indeed until quite recent times all land had to be rested for one or more years. Therefore there were probably few sites which saw permanent settlement in the early Iron Age. Succeeding generations moved up and down the Valley, burning off old scrubland and redigging field boundaries. Housing design had not advanced from the flimsy mud huts of preceding peoples, except that besides round huts, rectangular ones were also attempted; therefore subsequent excavation provides little evidence of occupation except for postholes, coarse pottery and animal bones. This apparent lack of concern for good living is not borne out by the care and expense lavished in decorating personal and domestic articles and weapons.

Three main waves of iron age settlement took place; the Hallstatt was followed by the noble La Tene culture, which produced a magnificent Celtic art form. Archaeology and accident have produced many fine examples from the bed of the Thames including the famous Battersea Bronze Shield, decorated iron swords and spearheads, and from Cookham a fine dagger with bronze open-work scabbard, only one of a number found in the river. Another find from the locality was a dug-out canoe, which may be attributed to the Iron Age, but of course, could be earlier. This was raised from the river-bed near Bourne End railway bridge in 1871. It was 25 ft. 3 ins. in length and 3 ft. 4 ins. wide, with an upward curving bow and a square stern, and two seats had been carved out of the solid wood.

The third Iron Age invasion sometime during the 2nd century B.C. was by the Belgae, a great confederation of Celtic tribes from Gaul. They brought with them the trappings of the Greek and

Roman civilizations such as coinage and wheel-turned pottery but, more importantly, they brought the heavy plough and durable iron farming implements, billhooks, sickles and other tools which differed little from the styles of today. Despite some resistance from the hillfort strongholds, the Belgae quickly conquered south-east England and by the time of the Roman invasion of 54 B.C. the area to the north of the Middle Thames was held by a tribe called the Catuvellauni, and to the south by the Atrebates, with the river forming the boundary between them.

In this first campaign Julius Caesar advanced across the Thames and captured the Catuvellauni oppidum at Wheathamstead in Hertfordshire. This was only a temporary conquest and after exacting tribute the legions departed. It was not until 43 A.D. that the more permanent conquest began. By then the Catuvellauni had moved their capital to Colchester and extended their territory over most of South East England by subjugating the Atrebates.

Although frequent tribal wars were waged up and down the Thames, men still had to earn their living from the land. This small district saw settlement throughout the Iron Age, with a scattering of small celtic fields and their accompanying farmhouses at Marlow, Cookham, Taplow and Maidenhead, as well as at the old established riverside site at Bray. Now the iron hand of Rome descended upon all; despite last ditch stands by Boadicea and her like, the Roman way of life was the way of every 'Romano-Briton' whether he liked it or not. Those who were lucky could carry on farming in the old-fashioned way as long as they paid their regular taxes in corn or livestock. Others were not so lucky, the young men were conscripted into the army and sent overseas or into slave gangs, labouring on the roads which began to open up the wildest regions of Britain. In many cases the local Belgic people were deprived of their traditional houses, which were replaced, often on the same site, by the Villas of the large farming estates which chequered the fertile lowlands through much of the Roman occupation.

Forest was cleared from some of the heaviest fertile soils which had previously been unworkable and large regular fields of waving corn sprang up to supply the insatiable demands of the tax gatherer, the army victualling officer and merchants from the growing towns. The soils to the south and west of Maidenhead saw little human habitation before the Roman occupation but then slave labour and improved farming techniques quickly carved out a pattern of estates with farmhouses or Villas at regular intervals of about 1½ miles. Other villas, such as at Castle Hill, Maidenhead, overlooked fields

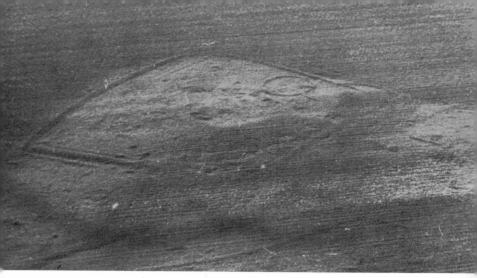

Cropmark of an ancient farmstead near Maidenhead

on the Thames Terraces and floodplain on which the modern town stands. Another less lavish farm existed at Cookham on top of a Belgic site, and there were others at Marlow, Bourne End, Hedsor and Taplow.

The Romans had a great deal of experience of inland navigation and were prepared to build canals where necessary. The natural Thames, however, was easily navigable by shallow draughted vessels and was a convenient highway for bulk cargoes of grain to be taken to Londinium from large specialized farms such as Hambleden, not far above Marlow. Vessels also shipped produce from a new wharf at the age-old riverside settlement at Bray, which was very convenient to the series of Villas near Maidenhead. The Bray settlement was in use for much of the period of Roman occupation and possibly into the 5th century A.D., well beyond the time when the legions withdrew, after decades of internal strife and continuous pressure on all sides from the pagan Germanic seafarers, Angles, Saxons and Jutes.

Local societies have recently shone a little more light on the dark age settlement of the Middle Thames region. The upper levels of the Romano-British site at Bray have produced scraps of Saxon pottery which may point to friendly settlement by Saxon mercenaries, who were initially on the side of the native population, or an early waterborn incursion by a hostile band. As with previous invasions, the Thames provided easy access into the heart of the country as they rowed up the river. The Saxon voyagers must have come up against

29

Upper Thames Cottage 1794

many punitive attacks by native Arthurian style heroes. At least a
dozen Saxon weapons of war have come from the riverbed between
Marlow and Maidenhead and Sashes Island, Cookham, has produced many so called Roman skeletons and iron weapons which
may be relics of one such clash. Likewise, less than a mile upstream
on the floodplain at Cockmarsh, a Saxon was interred in a Bronze-
Age burial mound, whilst nearby on the crest of a hill overlooking
the river, six Saxon warriors were laid to rest, each with his sword,
spear and shield by his side.

By the end of the 6th century most of Southern England was in the
hands of the Anglo-Saxons and large scale migration brought a new
race of farmers to the Thames Valley. Archaeological traces of
Saxon settlements are just as elusive as those of their predecessors.
The ordinary people lived in squalid huts with floors sunk below
ground level, whilst on a permanent site the head man may have

30

resided in a large wooden rectangular hall. Many of the smaller *Grubenhauser* have been found on the Upper Thames gravels, but none so far in Middle Thames region. This state of affairs may shortly be rectified owing to the exciting discovery by the Maidenhead Society of a wooden structure at Braywick dating from the 8th century. The majority of local villages are of Saxon origin, therefore the scanty remains of the first settlements would have been swept away by later buildings.

Taplow, of course, has provided us with a Saxon structure in the form of Taeppa's burial mound, sited on top of an impressive chalk cliff overlooking the river. The mound was hacked open in 1883 by an enthusiast whose local operations are now viewed with either amusement or horror. Despite the lack of expertise of the diggers, the surviving material from the grave, now dated to about 620 A.D., justly deserves its position in the British Museum as one of the most precious collections of Anglo-Saxon art to be found in England. Apart from the obvious use of the river as a highway, other evidence leads us to conclude that the original founders of Cookham and other nearby villages were family groups who migrated up the Thames Valley from parent settlements in Kent. Kentish style objects from Saxon graves in this area include a bronze two-handled basin from the warrior group above Cockmarsh and a circular gold pendant from an isolated grave at High Wycombe. Other evidence is revealed in later records concerning Medieval Cookham, for it would appear that some local names and terms used in 13th-century manor accounts have Kentish connotations.

The impression one gets from the Anglo-Saxon Chronicle covering the five hundred years up to the Norman conquest is one of continuous strife, towns and monasteries sacked with monotonous regularity, with petty Kingdoms, alternately Christian and Heathen, dominant for a time and then crushed by more vigorous invaders. In fact the age was also one of steady settlement, when towns such as London, Wallingford and Oxford grew in importance, and when most of our villages were founded. Some of the earliest, with place names ending in 'ham' (village) are concentrated along the east and south coasts, in Kent and Surrey, and along the banks of the Thames where twenty-five per cent have the suffix 'ham'; Fulham, Laleham, and of course, Cookham, or as it was in the 8th century, Coccham — a village and manor by no means unique but one with a rich local history which can be used as an example of the growth of many such villages whose inhabitants moulded the English landscape.

It is said that at one time there was a monastery at Cookham, if so

31

it did not last for long, probably suffering the fate of many others on one of the several occasions when the Danes rampaged up and down the Valley. The Manor of Cookham passed to the Crown in Edgar's reign and was important enough for a meeting of the Witan, the King's Council, to take place there during the reign of Ethelred the Unready. There was some setback to the development of the village at the time of the Norman Invasion when lives may have been lost and property forfeited, but together with the neighbouring settlement of Bray, at the time of the Domesday Survey of 1086, Cookham had recovered to become a thriving township and could even boast a market. The village of wooden houses, probably set within exactly the same boundaries as it is today, contained about sixty families each entitled to farm a certain number of strips in the great open fields which stretched over the fertile terraces to the south. On either side of the village, on the land liable to winter flooding, were the lush pastures and meadows for the grazing of sheep and cattle and for the support of the oxen; five or so plough-teams, with eight oxen to a plough.

Thanks to the stalwart villagers of more modern times these commons remain, in the shape of Cockmarsh and Widbrook (originally Withie Brook) Commons.

On the higher ground to the west there began the ancient woodlands, Heysulle and Inwood, in which the villagers had the right to collect *cablish*, wind-blown branches, one of the few sources of fuel. There were also rights of pannage, whereby the stock, particularly pigs, could forage for beech mast and acorns, at certain times of the year. The Manor also held rights of pannage at Benefeld (Binfield) and Sunigehulle (Sunninghill) some distance away in the heart of Windsor Forest. These rights may have gone back to family connections in the days of the original settlement of the area. The King's hunting forest lay all around, stocked with deer and other beasts of the chase. The thickets held dangers to the unwary, for wild boar and wolves still roamed the countryside.

The Church at Cookham, before and after the Norman conquest, was held by Reinbald, Chancellor to Edward the Confessor. He also held one and a half hides of arable land, probably scattered strips within the common fields, tilled by eight humble cottagers each with one ox which together made up their plough team. Reinbald also held hides of land in Bray and further down river at Boveney. The record also says that he held Cannon Court Farm on the outskirts of Cookham Manor. All these lands passed to the Abbey of Cirencester in the reign of Henry I.

Adjoining Cannon Court at the time of the Domesday Survey was another small estate of three hides, called Elentone, which at the Conquest had been given to the Norman family of de Pynkenye, presumably for services rendered to King William during the invasion. The nearby hamlet of South Elentone or Ellington which grew up in the 12th century, eventually became Maydenhuth, the modern Maidenhead. Recently, five years of archaeological work on the moated site of Elentone, latterly a manor of the de Spencers and now known as Spencers Farm, gave an intimate view of the way of life of estate bailiffs from the 11th to the 15th centuries, and if this was the way of life of persons of comparative affluence then God must have helped the poor peasants!

In the late Saxon period an artificial mound had been raised on low ground near the Withiebrook, a floodplain stream. The first building was probably a rectangular wooden hall built around a series of large posts sunk deep in the ground. This was superseded in later centuries by one or more timber-framed Long Houses erected on roughly mortared flint foundations. Each house was strictly open plan, being no more than an open hall bisected at one end by a 'screens' passage, with a small buttery beyond. Near the middle of the hall lay the fireplace, a simple flat hearth made of tiles set on edge in typical medieval fashion. There was no chimney, smoke escaped through the ends of the tiled roof. The floor consisted of nothing more than crushed chalk probably covered in rushes. Over three centuries or more it rose considerably in height for when one chalk layer became full of scraps of broken crockery and other items, and was too uneven and filthy to walk upon, another was laid on top. From the screen's passage a door led to the kitchen area in the backyard. Here lay the cooking hearths, bakehouse and two wells, one probably replacing the other when it became sour.

The rubbish of centuries littered the site, for there had been no attempt to keep kitchen refuse away from the mound. Most of the animal bones not consumed by domestic pets were trodden into the ground or thrown into the surrounding ditches. In the case of something exceptionally large such as the skull of a horse, a hole was sometimes dug to receive it. During the whole of the excavation only two or three coins of the period were found, for up to the 16th century money was of little importance, most trading being done within the barter system. Yet we can see that at times the household was reasonably affluent by the standards of the period. Among the hundredweights of coarser domestic cooking pottery there was plenty of the finest tableware, well glazed and decorated, fit for a knight and his lady when they came on a tour of the estates.

A mile or so away on the other side of their open fields, the Coo-

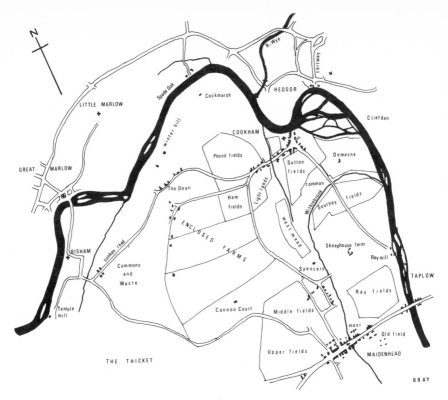

Map of the fields of Cookham and Maidenhead in the 17th century

kham villagers on one of His Majesty's own demesnes, were in a favoured position. They did not pay geld and could expect to receive fairer justice than many bound to lesser masters. After King William built the first motte and bailey castle at Windsor there were even closer ties with the Crown. As the castle grew in magnificence under successive monarchs the profits and produce of the manors of Cookham and Bray, with the Seven Hundreds of the forest area, went towards the upkeep of the castle household and even towards major construction work.

The constable of the castle was also keeper of the King's forest and bailiff of Cookham and Bray, renting the manors direct from the King. The bailiff could be commanded, out of issues of his bailiwick, to pay for such things as the painting of the King's chapel and the building of apartments for the Queen. On the other hand when in 1224 Henry III wanted extra stocks of corn from the two manors, the

34

Monarch had to pay for them. Early in the 15th century the inhabitants complained that the manor profits were being embezzled by individuals, but in 1450, one hundred marks per annum were still being charged upon the manors for castle maintenance.

In the 13th century the bailiff was required to submit to the King's Treasurer detailed accounts of manor profits and expenses. As constable of the castle he was not often at the manors but acted more like a tenant-in-chief, leaving others in direct control. Among them was the reap-reeve, who allotted the tasks of the serfs working on the King's land, for the majority of villagers, the villeins, not only had to work their own strips but had also to cultivate their Lord's demesne lands for perhaps three days in every week. The lowly cottars with only a few acres of their own, hired out their services for their keep to the more prosperous villeins and later to the "freemen" when they began to rent separate farms from the King.

Below the reeve was the bedell or hayward, who was responsible for the upkeep of the meadowlands. Whole families were employed at busy times of the year, particularly harvesting, when they were provided with food and beer. Other officials in Cookham and Bray were the foresters and the 'Soigeant' or constable who received a stipend of a penny a day. Other workers vital to the smooth running of the community but without time or land enough to grow their own produce were also partly or wholly supported by the manor. These included the blacksmith who received the customary pig each year and the dairymaid who not only received an annual stipend but occasionally, as in 1246, was allocated, together with the bedel, five quarters and four bushels of mixtilion, mixed grain, for the making of coarse bread.

The dairy was of considerable economic importance to the manor, for the lush riverside meadows provided good summer grazing, yielding an excellent milk supply. The issues for the year 1288 included such items as twenty eight gallons of milk sold outside the manor at a halfpenny per gallon, and twelve and a half gallons of butter at sixpence per gallon. The same year a weigh and a half of cheese was sold for twelve shillings, containing sixty cheeses, "so many cheeses because small", and another batch of four and a half weighs which made one hundred and twenty seven cheeses, fetching forty-five shillings. This appears to have been a particularly good summer, for the manor was also able to sell a large quantity of hay. Other profits were made on poultry, "price of a cock a penny-farthing and of a hen a penny-halfpenny" and eighty stickes of eels from the fisheries, each sticke of twenty-six fetching fourpence halfpenny.

Owing to the general absence of winter fodder much of the livestock was usually sold or slaughtered at the end of the year, so it is not surprising to find among the accounts for 1246 a receipt for "12 cows, 22 bullocks, 23 calves sold for want of forage £12 11s. 10d." Profits came from many other sources; fines from the Manor Court, Herbage and Pannage in Binfield and Sunninghill, cablish and honey, hides, sheep-skins and wool, also plough shares and horse-shoes were made at the smithy. The "issues of the barn", rye, barley, oats, wheat and peas were being produced in large quantities, flour and malt came from the mill and in one year the large sum of £12 was made on "Old Oaks sold of the Kings Demesne Wood".

On the debit side, several tons of oats and lesser quantities of other cereals had to be bought each year, for seed and fodder was sometimes required to get the valuable plough oxen through the winter. If the winter was particularly severe, not only did the people go hungry but much of the stock perished, often leading to a heavy bill for new oxen as well as the usual sheep and cattle re-stocking in the spring. Lesser bills had to be paid for labour on routine repairs to the wood-work of the larger houses and to the mill and weirs and on land maintenance such as the carting of dung, the rebuilding of walls, hedging and ditching. Apart from perhaps salt for perserving fish and meat and iron and steel for essential tools, little else had to be bought outside the manor.

Life on the manor changed little over hundreds of years, although after the Black Death the resultant labour shortage in the 15th century brought about a slight improvement in the life of many peasants. The manorial system was breaking down and people were no longer tied rigidly to one lord but could come and go as they pleased. Gradually the forest had been cleared back and new enclosed farms were appearing on the edge of the mother settlement, maybe depriving the villagers of forest rights but yielding valuable new rents to the lord. Until the revolutionary enclosures of the 18th and 19th centuries people generally carried on with the same farming methods, with the same hand-to-mouth existence of their Saxon forebears. Life was hard but the villagers were basically self-sufficient.

The Manor Court was held at regular intervals to deal with the complicated business of leases and tenancies and providing a rough but usually fair justice before a jury or 'homage'. Ordinary villagers could obtain redress even from knights and lords.

Across the river in the tiny manor of Hedsor, the Court Rolls of the Tudor period provide us with further glimpses of the unchanging life of the inhabitants and examples of the many day-to-day problems which arose, such as the disposal of stray sheep and other animals. A most comical item of this nature (in 1605) is as follows:- "The Homage present that two mares of Robert Webbe were impounded in the Lords pound at Hedsor, which said mares should have remained three or four days, the pound was broken and afterwards the mares were seen pasturing on Roberts land at Wooburne (the adjacent Parish) and that Robert, on the evening before the breaking of the pound wished to borrow a saw, but for what purpose the Homage are not thoroughly acquainted"!

All the villagers having strips in the open fields were also commoners, with jealously guarded rights of pasturage at certain times of the year on the stubble, meadows and waste. "No mares, sheep, cattle or hoggs shall pasture on Hedsor or Wooburn Meades from the beginning of mowing time until the meadows be cleared of all the hay. . .". Woe betide any other tenant who let his animals stray onto common land without permission, or conversely any tenant or freeholder who laid claim to the ownership of such lands:- "Whereas the inhabitants of the vills of Hedsor, Hicheham, and Tapley are, and from a time of the contrary whereof the memory of man is not, where intercommoners for all beasts, that is to say, for horses, cows, oxen, sheep and pigs on the wastes and woods of Hedsor, Hicheham and Tapley. Elizabeth Alforde unjustly demands 16 pence for every pig pasturing in the woods, whereas in truth they have not paid nor hitherto have they been wont to pay anything — 1582."

Tudor barn, White Place Farm 1974

In the 17th century we begin to see a breaking up of the ancient commons and waste. Under 'Queen Elizabeth's Law' cottages could sometimes be erected on the waste as long as they had four acres of enclosed land adjacent. The yearly rents were often purely nominal such as the traditional grain of pepper or perhaps "two pence and two fat capons on the day of St. Thomas".

Payments in the form of produce go back to the early Saxon period when the lower orders knew nothing of coinage, and although many were later commuted to cash payments much of the age-old customs lived on into the 17th century. The most interesting one from Hedsor concerned a property of over 100 acres at Lilley Fee in Wooburn which was held in free socage at a yearly rent of "23/11, one cock, two hens, one gallon of ale and two loaves by the year of human bread". At the manor court in July 1573 the tenant, Lambert Rydynge, did fealty to his lord and asked and was granted that beyond this service he might also keep for the lord at his own expense "one sparrow hawk and two hunting dogs called Spannielles", one imagines for his own use rather than his lord's! Seven years later the homage presented that Rydynge had "closed his last day" and as his son Thomas was only twelve years old his unfortunate widow Anne must pay the customary dues and still look after the "Sparhawk and Spannielles" and also "carry to the table of the Lord of the Manor the first dish of the second course at the Feast of the Nativity".

The ancient Royal Demesne of the Manor of Cookham consisted of about 400 acres of low gravel terrace and alluvium to the south of the village. In the common fields there were 336 acres of arable, at first made up of scattered strips, but later probably gathered into compact blocks, consisting of 68 acres in a furlong called Sutton, 58 acres in the Donne, 32 acres in the Hame, 95 acres in Handleigh and 83 acres in Eldfield. There was also considerable meadowland; 20 acres in Batlingmeade, 32 acres in the Marshe, 3½ acres in West Withiebrooke and 2 acres in Sydenham. Also included were the fisheries and a number of other lands and tenements with obscure names such as Penny Faders and Grom als Eyrome. A number of these were held in tenure by the long established Babham family so were probably situated in the area of Formosa Island and Odney.

The manor house of the Bailiff of Cookham was in the centre of an enclosed area of the Royal Demesne lands encompassing modern White Place Farm. The name probably originated with a Walter le White who held lands in Cookham in 1322. The Whites are mentioned in the Court Rolls of 1390 when they held "lands and meadows of the King or the Lady Queen of her manor of Cookham". In

1493 the manor passed from the Bullock family to William Norreys who was then the Royal Bailiff and whose family held many lands in the area. In 1536, at the death of Lionel Norreys without heir, it passed to the Fyfield branch of the family. John Norreys (probably the same John who was controller of the honour and castle of Windsor in 1555) was heir to the estate in 1562, holding "divers lands and tenements in Cookham of the Queen in Ancient Demesne". Later in the same year, John Cheyney admitted tenancy of the Norrye's lands in Cookham "being Bullocks, White Place, Shaseys (Sashes Island) and Bradleys". Four years later Cheyney sold the lease to Ralphe Moore for £300. In 1602 the Moores sold the estate to Widow Dorothy FitzWilliam who only held it for two years before selling to George Smyth Esq. Beside the arable and meadowlands, the estate then consisted of 8 messuages, 8 gardens, 8 orchards, 3 tofts, 1 dovecote, 10 acres of land covered with water, and a free fishery.

In 1611 there came a shrewd move by the powerful Manfield family, whose ancestors had held the Manor of Taplow, including Cliveden and Amerden from at least 1440, leasing it at first from Merton Priory and later Henry VIII. The Manor of Bullocks, alias White Place, lay on the opposite side of the Thames to the Manfield mansion on the Cliveden heights. Old Henry Manfield was often casting covetous eyes on the lush meadowlands across the water and it wasn't long before he noticed that George Smyth had an eligible daughter and he had a son. So the two estates became one at the wedding of young Sir Edward Manfield and Mary Smyth.

In 1638 the Exchequer Queen's Remembrancer, the official responsible for the collection of outstanding revenues due to the Crown, subpoenaed Sir Edward and other local gentlemen to declare what lands they held, for they appeared to have in their possession the greater part of the Royal Demesne land and meadows of Cookham. The reason for the sudden interest of Royal officialdom in its ancient property is not known, but it could be that Manfield and his like were indulging in a spate of land enclosure to improve their farming techniques, which naturally led to complaints by the villagers.

Manfield stated that the lands were his own free inheritance and denied that he owed rent and services to the Crown, but the reply of the Attorney General documented the extent of the demesne, and stated that Manfield owed the following ancient services as rent in kind, which even in the 17th century must have seemed ridiculously old fashioned.

"For White Place — 1 labourer to mow the Kings grass in the

Harvesting at Burnham 1880

Kings demesne meadows called Battlemead and the Marsh; 2 days.

2 labourers to make the Kings hay there 2 other days.

5 men labourers to reape the Kings corne of his demesne 2 days and they there to mowe the corn and carry with horse and carte 1 day.

The corne so reaped and mown another day, the hay as aforesaid.

To pay yearly unto ye Kings use 1 wheaten cake and 3 hens at the feast of St Michael, 40 sticks of eels at Lent and various other rents.

For Bullocks and Shawzies a like rent, excepting eeles."

In 1650 the Parliamentary survey of the whole manor commuted all rents to cash payments. Manfield was included in the list of freehold and copyhold tenants paying the princely sum of £4 17s. 7d. for all of Bullocks, Shawzies, etc.

In 1671 Sir Edward Manfield, now in his seventies, held many hundreds of acres of land, including the mansion and park at Cliveden, the manor of Amerden, property in Hedsor, Taplow, Hitcham and Dorney and wharfeage and towpath rights on the Thames. His Cookham properties were now described as the Manor or Farm of Bullox, or Bullocks, two pasture grounds called Little Bullox or Bullox Odney and the capital messuage or farm called White Place.

Despite all this Manfield had taken up considerable mortgages and was now in serious debt, owing Sir William Rawsterne £7,800.

In 1681 Manfield died, leaving his personal estate to Rawsterne and naming his executor. Unfortunately Rawsterne died the same year. George Villiers, second Duke of Buckingham had already agreed to purchase the estate, but he also died in a riding accident, leaving the intended estate to Mary, Duchess of Buckingham and his son, Sir William Villiers.

It seems that by 1680 Buckingham had already built the first of the known mansions on the present site of Cliveden House but his family neglected to pay for the estate until an enquiry in 1696. The High Court then ordered that the entire Manfield estate was to be auctioned, the moneys going to Dame Alice Rawsterne and other claimants. It was purchased in 1703 by Budd Wase, one of the claimants, for £17,200. Wase sold the Manor of Bullocks, alias White Place, the same year to John Dodson, a London Tinplate manufacturer. His daughter married a George Leycester and this family held it until 1893. In 1893 the White Place Farm and Cliveden Estates were bought by the Astor family. In 1942 the Third Viscount made over Cliveden to the National Trust, the following year giving covenants over 102 acres of White Place Farm.

Under the Tudors and Stuarts there was a steady rise in the population necessitating further land enclosure, so that improved farming methods could provide more food. Many peasants were now able to improve themselves, buying up blocks of land in the open fields or enclosing some of the forest lands and becoming wealthy farmers. Larger quantities of surplus produce from the Cookham farms could be sold at the local market in the growing town of Maidenhead.

Most of today's picturesque timber-framed country cottages were built in this period, not as humble dwellings for the labouring class but as refined residences for the new middle class of yeoman farmers and craftsmen. Their labourers, the cottagers, rented far inferior dwellings, living in primitive conditions which in some areas lasted into the 19th century. In Berkshire, cottages were then generally described as having ragged thatch or broken tiles, an earthen floor, the walls brown with smoke and frequently only one bedchamber for a numerous family. So life for the average peasant had changed little since Saxon times. In Cookham, those not already tied to the number of enclosed farms were able to carry on with remarkable tenacity the ancient farming methods on the lands of their Saxon forebears, until 1852, when the last of the open fields were enclosed.

By the beginning of the 19th century the Agricultural Revolution brought proper three and four year rotation of cereals, alternating with new crops such as potatoes and turnips, which had first come

Haymaking 1900

into use on the more efficient farms. However, on the common fields
rotation was still said to be irregular, and the ancient tools almost
identical to those used by the Romano-British farmers were still in
use. The lush meadows were cut by teams of men swinging long-han-
dled scythes, behind came the women and children, spreading the
hay to dry for several days, but returning each evening to rake it into
cocks, then when dry carrying it to the rick.

The heavier soils of the open fields were still ploughed into ridge
and furrow, sometimes by oxen, but more often by heavy horse
teams. Wheat was sown, broadcast and harrowed or ploughed in. At
harvest time farms employed whole families who began work at six
o'clock. A row of men moved ahead across the field, cutting the corn
with short sickles, keeping up a steady rythmn which had to be sustained for a back-breaking twelve hours. For this a man might earn
up to four shillings a day with free beer. The harvest gatherers, the
women, could earn a shilling a day and maintenance. However, it

Haystacks at Hedsor 1890

was thought to be rather a shame that fewer women worked on the farm as they could make more money, particularly in Marlow, by straw plaiting and lace making, and in Cookham from 1828, by making boots and shoes, a cottage industry which at one time employed 1,500 people. Apart from the paper mills the only other industries to provide work for the poorer classes were the sacking manufactory at Bray Workhouse and Taplow Cotton Mill, to which the poor children of Maidenhead went.

Besides the regular work in the fields there were many other jobs to be attended to throughout the seasons. In August, rushes had to be cut and dried for basketry and thatching. Osiers were also cut and prepared for basketwork. Willow trees, which lined every watercourse in the area, were of vast consequence in the business of a farm and were so highly valued that it was said that they "will purchase a horse, before an oak will find him a saddle". They were polled every 7 years and the timber was used for lathes, gates and hurdles. Hazel and coppice wood was also cut at regular intervals, providing timber for various needs around the farm and village, and sometimes sent to London as barrel hoops and brooms. Brushwood, turf and furze was collected for winter fuel, as only the wealthy could afford coal. A cottager worth his salt would invariably have a well-stocked vegetable

43

Marlow Regatta 1900

garden and a sty for the family pig, fed on kitchen scraps and anything else available, nothing being wasted. Chickens and ducks roamed free range, but were often kept within the cottage at night. Specialist breeders might keep several broods in the living room, with hens brooding ducks eggs in the bedroom.

At the beginning of the 19th century the town of Maidenhead, consisting of little more than 1,000 inhabitants, provided weekly marketing of cottage produce as well as large quantities of corn, sold by sample. Everyone went to the Maidenhead fairs at Whitsun or at the end of September and November, when there were great dealings in "all sorts of cattle".

A November cattle and horse fair was also held at Marlow, preceded by a rather dull pleasure fair, for "the countrymen herabout are not of a mirthful cast, and their liveliness is of a very laborious character". Not surprising when it was said that the houses about the meaner streets had a wretched poverty-stricken aspect and there were evident signs of vice forcing themselves on the attention!

At the time of "the prevailing disease" in 1831 (typhus or cholera, more prevalent in larger towns and cities), the townspeople, displacing country people living in cramped conditions, had to be taught that it was not a good idea to leave piles of old clothes lying about the room or to site cesspools, privies and pigsties by the backdoor. In the middle of the 19th century the Gas and Coke Company began to lay pipes for street lighting, while at the same time poor families of the parish, were allowed funds from the rates, administered under the Poor Law regulations, for emigration to Australia, the land of plenty.

Throughout the Victorian period the population of Marlow stagnated, and Marlow itself was described as a second-rate agricultural town, burdened with an expensive new bridge and church. The cattle fair was still well attended in 1899 and there was work in the paper mills, brewery and chair factory but the town was no longer a port of any great importance on the Thames. By the 1850s the trade in corn, coal and timber had fallen off so much that bargemaster William Sparkes had opened up as a beer retailer at *The Barge Pole* in Church Passage, St. Peter's Street. Thirty years later *The Barge Pole* was run by Mrs. Maria Sparkes but was now called *The Fishermans' Arms*. This graphically illustrated the changing fortunes of river and town from commerce to pleasure, for the commercial wharf had been replaced by a boatyard hiring out craft to the gentry who came down for the trout fishing. Many decided that Marlow was a nice place for retirement, which was good news for the shopkeepers.

Maidenhead, on the other hand, had always been a bustling town, full of hostelries and shops, catering for the coach trade on the Bath Road. Then Brunel brought the railway, shortly to be followed by the Victorian builders, reaching out speculative fingers into the neighbouring parishes. The population of 1,000 in 1800 had reached 3,300 by 1841, almost doubling thirty years later and reaching 13,000 by 1910.

Cookham, however, despite the battering of commercialism on its doorstep, managed to last as a comparatively unchanged village community until the early years of the 20th century. There was industrial work at the brick and tile works and paper mills, but the main interest was still farming. 'Blackbird' Hatch (he never stopped whistling) tended the sheep on the commons of Cookham Dean, sometimes ferrying the flock over the Thames to pasture on the Little Marlow Meadows. The smith and farrier had work in plenty, likewise the thatcher, hedger, gamekeeper, laddermaker, hurdlemaker and the workers of the land. They and their families although of lowly station, lived the contented life of most country people, for they were at one with the land, they knew its worth and believed it to be permanent.

2 · THE FISHERIES

Primitive man evolved some ingenious devices for catching fish. Many ancient types of nets, traps and lures are still in use on streams and rivers all over the world. Some types used on the Thames only died out in the first half of this century. Throughout thousands of years the people of the valley relied heavily on fish to subsidize their diet. Mesolithic man used hooks, lines and harpoons, very much like the Eskimos, and although there is no evidence to prove it, he probably also used nets and basket-traps.

Fish weirs must have come into use at a very early stage. For the first time the hand of man affected the current and course of the river. Early weirs, which were called Kidells, Hedges or Stops in medieval times, were rough brushwood structures fixed to the river bed by piles. They were constructed across narrow channels at islands, or partially across the main river, and were angled across the current in the shape of a shallow 'V' or 'W'. Migrating fish were funnelled into the open apex of the 'V' in which were set large nets or baskets.

Kidells were used up until Tudor times. They undoubtedly made a substantial profit for the owner, usually the Lord of the Manor, or local Abbot, but over the centuries they became more and more of a hindrance to the increasing river traffic. As early as 1066 Edward the Confessor is reported to have passed an act relating to the four Royal rivers, Thames, Trent, Severn and Yorkshire Ouse. It stated:- "If mills, fisheries or any other works are constructed to their hindrance, let these works be destroyed, the waters repaired, and forfeit to the King. . ." Dozens of acts were passed throughout the centuries, but the fishery owners were usually also in control of local law enforcement, so naturally very little was done to clear the navigation channel.

The first lightly built weirs gave way to more substantial structures. Double rows of interlaced piles were set across the river, the space between the rows being filled with hurdles and general rub-

Raising eel bucks

bish. Many of them would have collapsed in the first winter spate, throwing debris and stones into the navigation channel and a mass of logs and branches against the next obstruction downstream.

In 1287, Bailiffs' accounts for the Manor of Cookham mention that eight pence was spent on rods for making a 'Burrock' for taking fish at the mill. The same year, a profit of three shillings and tenpence was made on fish caught at the mill. This was a substantial sum in those days, but far greater was the thirty shillings which was obtained in that and other years for "eighty stikkes" of eels, at four-pence-halfpenny a stikke. A stikke contained twenty-six eels. This points to the fact that there was a thriving industry in eels here and possibly on many other parts of the river by this time. A separate structure for catching eels was now in use. A Buck was a huge basket made of willow rods, and had undoubtedly been used in some form or other in Celtic times. In construction and name it closely resembled the Butt or Putt of the Severn district.

48

Laying grigwels

Many sets of eel-bucks were still used on side channels of the main
river into the 20th century. There were usually six or seven bucks to a
stage, with the open ends of the baskets, up to ten feet in diameter,
facing upstream. Side chambers were provided at the lower ends of
the baskets, into which captured eels found their way out of the rush
of the main current. Bucks were normally used from October to
December, during the main migration run to the sea. In 1875 a good
night's take from one stage could exceed half a hundred-weight of
fish, fetching about a shilling per pound. Galvanized iron baskets
were then replacing the traditional wicker-work. Other types of fish
traps were widely used from prehistoric until recent times. In the
18th century, prices of fishermen's gear included fishpots at one shilling, grigpots or wels also one shilling, clear wels at two shillings and
sixpence, and Bucks at five shillings each.

During the six to ten years that eels 'grow up' in inland waters,
they are usually called green or yellow eels, but on the Thames they

are 'Grigs'. Therefore grigwels or 'weels' were used throughout the year except when the fish, then called silver eels, were migrating to the sea. Weels were long, narrow necked wicker baskets, made of willow rods. They were laid on the river bed with their open ends facing downstream, in sets of eighteen or so, and left overnight baited with offal or gudgeon.

For thousands of years the tasty and nutritious eel has been on the diet in many European countries, although it seems to have lost its popularity in recent years. Maybe they are not so common as in the past, certainly not many are caught with rod and line, but this is mainly because they are noctural feeders. Also pollution in the estuary may have stopped the elvers ascending the river. Gone are the days when every seven years or so at Teddington a black ribbon of thousands upon thousands of elvers worked their way upstream, climbing over every obstruction, including the lockgates. Every small boy in the neighbourhood came to gather the harvest, which was made into eel-cake.

Our forebears ate many other species of coarse fish. There are remains of many fishponds, especially for carp, all over the country. Izaac Walton says a tasty dish can be made even of the chub, but his recipe included plenty of herbs, butter and salt, otherwise the flesh has been likened to muddy cotton wool full of needles! The humble gudgeon makes an excellent pie, which is probably still to be had in country districts. Other small fish such as roach, dace and bleak, are good fried, and tasty perch were canned in large quantities during the Second World War and sold as 'Perchines'. The pike makes one of the best meals of the lot and is still widely eaten by the coarse fishing fraternity. It is still extensively farmed on the Continent.

All the coarse fish are still abundant in our river, perhaps overabundant and therefore stunted from lack of food. Trout are less common. Some monsters exist in main river weir pools where the water is highly oxygenated, but largely the species keeps to the purer tributaries. The River Wye in Bucks was such a tributary until the 19th century. Up until the 1830s, eight to ten trout, weighing up to six pounds each, could be rod caught at one session. But by the 1850s chemicals from the paper mills had polluted the stream. On top of that, many fish of all sizes were killed off by poachers pouring bleach into the water.

In 1875 large conical Hoop-Nets were still being used to catch general fish, sometimes even ensnaring an unwary otter. As the name suggests, the hoop-net consisted of a large wooden hoop, up to six feet across, from which a long conical string net trailed to a point. It

Hoopnets

was lowered and pegged to the river-bed from some sort of light staging. The entrance probably faced downstream.

The other net commonly used was the Seine. This was used wherever the river was wide enough and clear of obstacles, mainly in the lower reaches and tideway. Seine netting is still commonly used around our coasts, principally for inshore fish such as bass. A very long net, deep enough to reach the sea bed is paid out from a rowing boat, one end of the net being fixed to the shore. The boat makes a semi-circle back to the shore and the ends of the net are pulled in, beaching any fish it has encircled.

The Thames was once our greatest salmon river. The story about the London apprentices refusing to eat salmon on every day of the week has been told many times. In the 18th century the banks of the river at London were strung with fishing communities. One can imagine the scene, say at Strand-on-the-Green. Long heavy rowing boats and punts drawn up above the tide-lines, seine nets, corks on one edge, weights on the other, drying in the breeze; women cleaning and packing the catch or mending nets. Hobbs was one noted fisherman on Chelsea Reach. He would take twenty fish in one haul. He probably obtained his nets in Fenchurch Street, where the net maker was paid eight hundred pounds a year for Thames salmon nets. Further up on the middle river, one hundred miles from the sea, professional fishermen on the famous Cliveden Reach were taking about fifty salmon each in a year. From this it can be seen that the number of fish ascending the river was very great, because they had to run the gauntlet of weirs, nets and traps on every mile of their journey to the spawning beds in the tributaries.

During the second half of the 18th century there was a gradual decline in the number of fish being taken, which coincided with the build-up of untreated effluents on the tidal river. This was brought about by the industrial revolution, which encouraged a movement of people from the country to London and other cities. Main drainage had yet to be invented and traditionally all waste products and sewage were dumped into the nearest stream. Normally natural agencies in the water soon broke down and absorbed any harmful pollutants but rapid urbanisation and industrial growth meant that waste was now pouring into the rivers in unprecedented quantities, too large to be purified naturally.

In 1857 an article was published in the Records of Bucks entitled "Remarks on the former abundance and present non-existence of salmon in the River Thames", by George Venables, incumbant of St. Pauls, Chatham. George was probably related to the Venables family who owned local mills. He says, "There are no places of sufficient size upon the banks of the Thames to injure (the young salmon) very much by sewage until it reaches London but having swept along, its graceful way clear and sparkling . . . a fitter river for the King of Fish than any other in Great Britain . . . it is received at the grandest city in the world by constant salutes of filth and sewerage . . . . These constant streams of filth flowing into the river, thrown back continually by the tide, reduce the Thames from a fine salmon river into a mass of moving mud, tossed about and prevented from depositing itself by the constant agitation of steamboats".

Venables' article includes "an account of all the salmon caught at Boulters Lock and the continguous part of the Thames from 1794 to 1821, both years included that is to say twenty-eight years or seasons", written by an un-named professional fisherman of Maidenhead. The journal, written by a man who also cut the local osier beds, and whose father was a Cookham fisherman, gives interesting details about fishing methods and tells of the last salmon caught at Maidenhead.

Fish were caught by netting in the weir and lock pool, or accidentally when they were drawn back into the eel bucks whilst leaping the weir. In 1796, for example, "We caught eight in the lock pool, and ten in the bucks; not one in the buck pool, for this year the buck pool was productive of nothing but great stones and hangings". By now the salmon was on the decline and the average annual catch up to 1800 was only twenty. The scarcity value is reflected in the price obtained, some fish fetching five shillings per pound. However, 1801 was an exceptional year, with sixty-six fish, weighing a total of 1,124 pounds, the largest 37 pounds. The price that year dropped to two shillings and sixpence per pound. Another very good year was 1804 with sixty-two fish, but after this the decline continued. The price rose to six shillings a pound in 1806, although one fish was spoiled by going to London by slow coach and instead of fetching six shillings it fetched only two shillings per pound. In 1808 there were only five fish; "caught one in the second buck at the (flash) lock, weight 18lbs., sold at 8s. per lb . . . . This was the highest price we ever got for salmon". For the next ten years the numbers fluctuated from eighteen to four, until in 1820 "not one caught by us, nor by any person within several miles". The final catches at Boulters came the following year, "two salmon were caught, weighing 18lb. and 13lb., the former on Tuesday, June 5th, and the latter July 13th".

Now after two centuries of pollution the problem is being tackled seriously, the tideway is being cleaned up and many species are once more surviving in the lower reaches. Let us hope that perhaps one day soon the salmon will again ascend the river on their way to ancient spawning beds.

From the time of Edward the Confessor until the 18th century, many acts were passed to try to control the number of obstacles to navigation, such as fishing and mill-weirs. Even a clause in Magna Carta called for "all Kidelli to be put down on Thames and Medway". Attempts were also made to preserve fish stocks. In 1287 an act of Edward I laid down a close season on all rivers and forbade the taking of young salmon on pain of imprisonment, and the burning of nets. Fifty years later there came complaints that fishermen on the River Thames, keepers of weirs, sluices and piles fixed across the river, and millers, took fish great and small and young by nets made with too narrow meshes and the weirs made for mills were so raised and obstructed the stream that the surrounding land was often flooded.

Further acts followed, mostly ineffectual. Interesting details of fishing methods are given in an act of Queen Elizabeth I in 1558. This laid down a minimum size limit of sixteen inches for salmon, eight inches for trout, ten inches for pike and twelve inches for barbel.

Fishing with rod and line always took second place to commercial trapping interests. Indeed there was a time when it was banned altogether at one place on the Thames. In the Cookham Court Rolls of 1556 "It is commanded to all the inhabitants within this manor and to all other persons that they shall not fish with hooks in any places in the Thames being about Cookham and Maidenhead, nor take fish with the hooks aforesaid unlawfully after the pain of 40d." From the days of Izaac Walton until well into the last century, the sport or art of angling was an indulgence which could only be afforded by gentlemen of leisure. Ordinary people were too busy trying to stay alive to be bothered with such a time-wasting and chancy sport. Now there are thousands upon thousands of match and pleasure anglers, using a basic method which is ten thousand years old.

The Cookham fisheries were set in a part of the Thames which was contained within the ancient Parish boundary, that is from Winter Hill below Marlow, to Maidenhead Bridge. Their history of the fish-

Cutting osiers

Peeling osiers

eries is long and complicated by the fact that many local names mentioned in the records were often spelt in different ways throughout the centuries, or the same place may have had several different names as one owner succeeded another. In early times maps did not exist and the extent of a fishery was passed on by word of mouth, therefore legal transactions at a later period had to rely on depositions of witnesses from the local population.

The fishery produced other things besides fish. Of almost equal importance was the cropping of osiers or 'withies' on the riverbanks and islands which were an integral part of the lease. Islands being the favourite sites for osier beds as there was no need to fence them against cattle. A sure and profitable annual return was made on the crop as it was essential to the local community for everything from wattle for house building to all types of basketwork. The cuttings were planted out in 'bolts' or 'hams' or prepared ground in February or March and the long slender withies cropped at about the same time, during the following year. The rods were winched into tight bundles called Luke, Threepenny, Middleborough, Great, according to length, and stood in water until they began to bud. They were then peeled in a 'break' and rebundled for sale. Well established willow trees also provided useful wood and were periodically polled. One can see the remains of many crumbling away on the riverbanks through lack of their traditional treatment. The willow has been extensively farmed well into this century but with the advent of cheap plastics the making of baskets will soon become another of the dying rural crafts.

Other crops within the fishery were partridge, pheasant, duck and water fowl of all kinds, for osier beds were ideal retreats and nesting places. In the water, crayfish were commonly trapped and fished, that is until a disease wiped out most of them on the main river at the end of the last century. Fortunately, however, they appear to be returning for there are at least two places where they have been caught in recent years.

The Domesday survey reported two fisheries in Cookham Manor, worth thirteen shillings and four pence. The next reference comes in the first Bailiff's accounts in 1246. The issues of the manor from this date until about 1320, include between eighty to ninety-two stikkes of eels each year, then worth up to forty-six shillings. Another "certain rent called Fispani" at eight shillings and eight pence also occurs. Also "for licence of fishing this year, twenty-four shillings and two pence". This last was for the fishery between Meydenhuth and Cogwell, first mentioned in 1287. In 1321 we have the first reference to the millpond fishery when the Bailiff "renders account of four pounds of the farm of one watermill with the fishery thereof so demised this year", also "thirty-five shillings of fisheries in the water of Thames and La Stonde by parcels this year demised". La Stonde was probably the separate floodplain stream, the name of which has been corrupted into Strand Water.

In Cookham Church there are several monuments to the Babhams. This ancient family is first mentioned in the accounts for 1355. "Henry de Babham gives to the Lord for a fine of one mark for the fishery of Cogwell", also William Casse and Thomas Waryn twelve shillings for Slogrove. In 1370, John Babham is "collector of the rent of the Lord the King", otherwise Bailiff, and "answers for forty-six shillings yearly of the farm of mill, fishery of the sluices of the same and pond of the same, together with profit of two small islands ajadcent so demised to William Hayle of Hurst for seven years". Cogwell (13 shillings and 4 pence), Slogrive (13 shillings and 4 pence) and La Stonde (2 shillings) were all held by John May.

56

In 1381 John Louche rented Cokewell, Slogrove and La Stonde, and John Chesk and William Fysshe the millpond. In 1465 a William Louches paid a new rent of sixpence a year for an island "between Tappeslow Myll and the bridge of Maidenhith". During this same year the tenures of Cokewell and Slogrove were demised to William Wyking. Ten years later the Bailiff answered for the whole of the fisheries still demised to Wyking. In this account it is amusing to see that he does not answer for the issues and profit of swans for they remain the use of the Queen, neither for issues of Herons and Shovelards (mallards) "for that none nested there", which I find hard to believe.

In 1542 the fisheries lease passed to Thomas Weldon, Chief Master of the Royal Household and later M.P. for Windsor, for the millpond "and several waters of the Thames", a very vague phrase which was to cause much trouble later, "and profits of two islands and osiers and willows, also Brewers Close and pasture of Queenleaze in the lordship of Bray, all parcel of escheated lands appurtaining to the lady Jane our late Queen of England". In 1559 there is a reference to the osier industry, when Ralph Moore who held Shaftseys (Sashes Island) by indenture of Lionel Norris, successfully prosecuted local fishermen, Roger and Stephen Holderness, for stealing twenty bundles of rods called cooper twigs from Shaftseys eyot.

A map of 1580-1600 shows "an eyot of Willows" and also has a Babhams Water, Kings Water and Fishing Stream and a Sashes Water. Hedsor and Pages Wharves are also marked, but the map is so crudely drawn that it is difficult to place any of the streams in their correct location. However, at the upper end of Sashes Island nearest to Cookham ferry, (now the bridge) there is drawn a long dog-legged structure running out halfway across the river towards the village. It is called the 'Warborough' and appears to have bushes growing on it. It may be concluded that this was an ancient fish weir which had reached a state of rustic permanence. Also marked nearby is the Headpile which marked the boundary between the fisheries. The name Warborough occurs quite frequently on the Thames. It has nothing to do with war but more likely derives from Weir or Ware, meaning an artificial bank.

The fishery lease passed from the Weldon family and was taken up by Edward Woodyer, passing to William Collins and Edward Fenn in 1631, when they also took over the Bray fishery from Maidenhead Bridge to Riddle Pool. The following year Richard Powney and John Phillips took over both leases. In 1633 the millpond changed hands yet again, passing to John Farmer of the Manor of Bradleys in Cookham. The extent of the fisheries was always worded vaguely in the legal documents and no maps were used; therefore it is not surprising that someone should argue over what he considered to be his rights. Farmer, probably quite correctly, assumed that the "several waters" mentioned with the millpond, in his and previous leases, meant the whole fishery in the Manor from Little Marlow Rails under Winter Hill to Maidenhead Bridge. What he did not seem to realise was that part of the river and a few small islands by Taplow Mill were outside the Cookham boundary and in the Manor of Taplow, for he claimed that Henry Guildford, who had held that Manor from 1605, and Thomas Hampson, who took it over about this time, farmed the islands and therefore owed him rent. Guildford replied that he had inherited Taplow Mill and estate, including a fishery and islands called Tynter Eyot, Ash Eyot, Gladmans Eyot and Normans Eyot, all of which he sold to Hampson. Hampson himself argued that legally Farmer only had the millpond fishery and that the Cookham boundary only extended halfway across the river, which Farmer flatly denied. All these proceedings were couched in the most complicated legal jargon, the term 'eyot' variously spelt ait, eit, eyt, and eight throughout.

Hampson now produced witnesses at an enquiry at Maidenhead to give the true extent of the fishery. The names include Parnell Chilburie, 77 year old wife of a Taplow Bargeman; 83 year old John Thackham of Burnham; Thomas War, millwright of Bray; William and Robert Sawyer, basket makers of Cookham, and John Byrde, fisherman, also of Cookham; they all stated more or less the same thing. Firstly there was an upper royal fishery from a furlong above Little Marlow Mead to a Great or Head Pile below Cookham Ferry. The millpond then ran from the Head Pile, between Bearleaze (now Odney Common) and Shawzies (Sashes Island) down to millbucks, rejoining the main stream at Pages Wharf. The third was called Islade, or Slogrove, extending from the upper end of Slogrove Mead (by My Lady ferry) to the lower end of Clemence, or Clemarsh Mead a furlong above Ray Lock, the ancient flashlock on the site of the modern weir. This fishery contained one ait, called Islake, near Babhams Bucks by Islade, and the other islands on Cliveden Reach called Slogrove. Taplow Mill Fishery went from Clemence Mead to the lower end of Taplow millpool and contained half of Headpile Ait within the Warborough, with two little meadows, one called Neate Hendge, two little tarries, Cherry Tree Ait, Flagg Ait and Teynter Ait adjoining Warborough. Maidenhead Bridge Fishery ran from

Peacocks Tarrs opposite Raymill to the bridge. This would therefore lie partly alongside and to the west of the Taplow Mill Islands and so be within the Royal Manor of Cookham. All this publicity resulted in an enquiry by the Attorney General, who decided that the aforesaid John Farmer and also Richard Powney, Bailiff of Cookham and Bray, had combined to defraud His Majesty of his fishings in the whole of the manor, when the lease was only intended to cover the Millpond. Farmer and Powney replied insisting that the "several waters" were included with it, the rent of the whole being 70 shillings and 8 pence, the millpond being only 6 shillings and 9 pence. Farmer now appears to have backed down regarding his claims over the Taplow Fishery, stating that he had Slogrove Fishery on the main river except:- "One island called Turners Mead, Cannon and Andrews eyts, and some eyts belonging to Taplow and Ray Mills, claimed by other persons and not this defendant."

In January 1635 a Berkshire inquisition of fifteen jurors reported officially on the extent of the Cookham fisheries. The limits of the upper and millpond fisheries were as deposed in 1633 but lower down things started to get complicated. The lower fishery is said to go down Slogrove to Maidenhead Bridge, the whole breadth of the Thames. The Islands mentioned lying in it from Clemence Mead downwards are Headpile or Normans, Turners Mead, Cannon Eyt, Peacocks Tarrs, Woodmancotes or Andrews Eyt, Queens Eyt, The "Oozy land" called Horneyard Tarr, Gladmans Eyt, Great and Little Tarrs, New Eyt with Longmeade Tarr, the Meade Plott of 2½ acres, Teynter Eiot, one eiot called Grasse Hill lying near the middle of the lower part of the several water by estimation two roods, and Maidenhead Bridge Eiot lying on the east side next to the bridge.

On 7th March that year Richard Powney was granted all the above, said to be worth thirty pounds but the rent remaining at 70 shillings and 8 pence. The following year (1636) he naturally took up the old complaint that he had not received back rent from 1631 for certain eyots near Taplow Mills. Hampson again defied him, insisting that they belonged to Taplow. He said the Inquisition wrongly named Peacocks Tarrs which should be Hornyett Tarrs, part of the islands, wharves, banks or Warboroughs of Taplow Mills, Queen Eiot should be Ashen, New Eiot should be Long or Thorne, part of Mill Meade, lately divided from the said Meadow by a hedge and dry ditch to save the osiers from "the spoyle of cattell". Grasse Hill should be Taplow or New Eyott and Maidenhead Bridge Eyott is only divided from Taplow by a ditch to protect the osiers from cattle on the common fields of Taplow.

There can be no doubt that the ancient Manor of Taplow must have established some sort of holding to a piece of valuable river frontage in Saxon times.

A plan of 1637 puts a lot of light on the position of the small islands. To the west of "the Lock" or flashweir, lie Ray Mill Close and Eyot. A further total of twenty-two islands stretches from Climarch to the bridge, most of which can be correctly identified, although duplication of names in the documents makes this rather difficult. The valuable osier plots are shown as separate islands but most had overfalls or shallows between them, otherwise the flashweir could not have maintained a head of water to operate Taplow and Ray Mills. The map is based on a copy of the original in the Public Records Office, made about the time of intensive investigations concerning the ownership of local lands and fisheries. The islands were named as follows:- (1) Climarch Mead, (2) Normans or Headpile, (3) Raye Eyote, (4) Turners Meade, (5) Faire Waie Tarrs, (6) Cannon Eyote, (7) Peacocks Tarrs, (8) Woodmancotes Eyote, (9) Queens or Ashen Eyote, (10) Horneyard, (11) Gladmans Eyote, (12) Little Tarr, (13) Great Tarr, (14) Teynter Eyote, (15) The Eight, (16) Flagge Eyote, (17) Cherry Tree, (18) Mill Meade, (19) New or Thorne Eyote, (20) Grasse Hill, (21) Raye Mill Eyote, (22) Raye Mill

Map of the Thames at Maidenhead in 1637

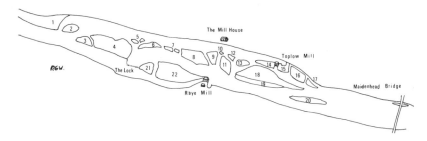

Lord Boston's eel bucks at Hedsor 1865

Close. At some later date the string of eyots adjoining Taplow Mill
Stream from Headpile to Mill Meade, were joined together by an
artificial bank. This must have improved the efficiency of the mill, as
a greater head of water could be maintained, but at the same time
any flood waters now coming down were all channelled into the modern weir stream, considerably increasing the speed of the current to
the bridge.

To return to the Cookham Millpond, in the latter part of the 17th century it is known as a free fishing Shawzies Water, which together with some lands in Cookham, formed part of the large estate of Sir Edward Manfield of Cliveden. Later, up to 1728, it was occupied by Richard Brown and Francis Sawyer, then passing to Jeffrey Wade and William Poulton. In 1739 Poulton bequeathed Shawzies to his son. A map of 1808 shows eel bucks still in the old position near the tail of the millpond in the possession of B. Witts Esquire.

To understand the geographical aspect of the old millpond fishery it must be remembered that man has considerably altered the several channels below Cookham Bridge. To begin with, prior to the mid-18th century the Lullebrooke stream between Odney Common and the village may have run in a channel further to the east. The usually accurate Rocque map of that time does not appear to show it in its present position, although it is mentioned by name in early records. Venables began the manufacture of paper at a mill on the site of the present mill house in the second half of that century, so the present channel may have been dug for that establishment. It is certainly on the Thames Commissioners' map of 1808.

This map shows that the ancient mill pond fishery was what is now called Odney Weirstream, together with another channel to the north which originally encircled two small islands and rejoined Odney stream near the present position of Odney Weir. This second channel was deepened in 1829-30 to form the upper portion of the lock cut, the lower half of which is completely artificial. At the same time much of the original land surface of Sashes Island was raised several feet by the excavated sand and gravels. The map gives Pages Wharf sited on the Buckinghamshire bank opposite the end of the lock cut and weir stream where they converge back into the main navigation channel. The wharf site is now occupied by the pictu-resque Ferry cottage nestling under the chalk cliff at the upper limit of the Cliveden estate.

A concrete structure still to be seen set into the riverbank about two hundred yards above the tail of Odney weir stream might have something to do with B. Witts' eel bucks. The medieval mill site was probably somewhere in this area. Just above here a deep silted-up channel leads south across Formosa Island. It is the most easily recognisable of several vague depressions which are all that remain of old channels shown clearly on the 18th century Rocque map.

The minor fishery of Hedsor Manor was situated on the old navi-gation channel, from what is now Cookham Upper Weir to the south-ern end of the Hedsor estate, below the site of the old eel bucks which belonged to Lord Boston in the last century. It was a minor fishery, because of necessity these interests had to take second place to the lucrative barge towing rights, which were usually held by the Hedsor Wharf tenant on this busy and hazardous section of the navigation.

Two weirs are mentioned in a litigation of 1360, and kiddels and fisheries in 1541. Thirty eight years later Hedsor Wharf was being sold to Rowland Hynde. In 1734 the Lord of the Manor leased the fishery to William Poulton who also had the wharf and "horsing" of barges. The lease was for twenty-one years at twenty pounds a year and "one couple of good capons of the value of three shillings, and in default three shillings in money and one dish of good and fresh fish of the value of three shillings on the first of May".

3 · WATER MILLS

From Neolithic times the quernstone was used to grind grain into flour and although the Romans are known to have introduced water milling into Britain, up to early medieval times the quern was the predominant tool for making bread. It was during the 8th century that water mills were re-introduced into eastern England and over the next few centuries a great number were built in all parts of the country, until by the time of the Domesday Survey in 1086 there were about six thousand. Thames mills were constructed at the "tail" or downstream end of narrow channels at islands, and sometimes new cuts were dug. As the river pushed down the dammed off millstream, a 'head' of water built up to work the mill wheel. Later, dams were thrown across any other adjacent channels to provide a greater head for extra power. Some of the old fishing weirs now went out of use as mill owners incorporated fish traps into their dams and sluices.

Early millers soon found themselves most unpopular as their dams began to cause flooding in the adjacent countryside. So it was not long before movable weir tackle came into use, to be lifted out at high water times and closed-in when the 'head' water was dropping off. Weirs had now to be constructed strongly and carefully, so that they controlled the water effectively and were not swept away. It is probable that the first simple design, the 'paddle and rymer', was identical to the one still in use on some Thames weirs today.

Basically, an even cill made of stone blocks or heavy timbers was fixed to the river bed the full width of the channel. The cill was held in place by vertical piles driven into the river bed at intervals. The piles also supported a catwalk across the river, several feet above high water levels. Supporting piles and cross timbers kept the whole structure rigid. The tackle consisted of removable squared piles, called rymers, set vertically into slots on the upstream edges of the cill at intervals of about two feet. The intervening gaps between the rymers were filled by square or oblong boards called paddles, laying across the rymers. There might be two or three paddles one above the

Primitive overfall weir at Hurley c. 1860

other, reaching from the cill to the head water level. There would be
many such 'sets' on a weir, depending on the width of the channel.
The paddles were each fixed rigidly to the end of a long pole rising
above the catwalk, so that they could be shut in or lifted out as
required. Paddle and rymer weirs covered the full width of the channel on the narrow reaches but on the middle and lower river they
were incorporated into mill-dams, overfalls or 'lasher' weirs, lashers
being lengths of timber laid horizontally along an overfall to increase
water levels.

Heavy tackle in the form of large wooden sluice gates hung on
chains worked by a winch was used to control the mill race. This was
later incorporated into some of the larger weirs and is still used in
some form or other on many weirs today. These large sluice gates,
some now made of iron, are called Bucks. This term originally
applied to the eel baskets, which were let down into the water in the
same way as sluice gates.

All early water mills were constructed entirely of wood. Even the
cogs and gears which turned the millstones and worked the hoists
had wooden teeth. Skilled millwrights probably had servicing con-

65

tracts and went from one manor to the next, seeing that all was running smoothly. It was not until as late as the 18th century that metal was introduced in the form of cast iron waterwheels. Generally, the simple basic design of buildings and machinery changed little over many centuries. Gradual improvements did, of course, take place and more power was created.

The six thousand watermills in England, recorded at the time of Domesday, had more than trebled in number by the 18th century, and the industrial revolution produced many more. In the Thames catchment area most were situated on the fast-running tributaries, there being about one hundred sites in Berkshire alone. On the main river there are roughly about forty sites which could have been used at one time or another. Many pre-date the Domesday Survey and only fell into disuse at the end of the last century, from Saxon to modern times they had served the local communities for a thousand years.

For the major part of this time the grinding of cereals was the chief function, but as the time of the industrial revolution approached, other uses were made of the power they created. Fulling mills were on the scene at an early date and mechanical devices such as hammers, presses and stirrers were invented and installed in the more powerful mills for the production of cloth, paper and various metal goods. One such mill was at Temple near Marlow. The name of Temple derives from the Knights Templar who held the Bisham estate from the 12th century. They, and later the Augustine monks of Bisham Abbey, held Temple Mills with the estate and undoubtedly used them for corn milling.

From about 1710 a company was producing "Bisham Abbey battery work", brass kettles and pans. According to Defoe c.1724, there was a foundry to convert copper into brass, which was then cast into large plates before being beaten by hammers into the required shapes. The company was doing well until "they turned into what they call a bubble, brought it to Exchange Abbey, set it a stock-jobbing in the days of our South Sea madness, and brought it up to be sold at one hundred pounds per share, whose intrinsick worth was perhaps ten pounds, 'till with the fall of all those things together, it fell into nothing again". The company appears to have survived, for brass and copper pans and kettles were being produced in 1748.

In 1788 the Mills were bought by The Copper King, Thomas Williams, M.P. for Marlow, who sparing no expense, brought in architect Samuel Wyatt to design new additions to the mill buildings. At the same time Wyatt designed a luxurious Thameside mansion and Marlow Town Hall which Williams gave to the town. Williams had extensive mining interests in Anglesea and smelting works in Swansea and according to the "General View of the Agriculture of Berkshire" (1810), made full use of the Thames and Severn Canal which opened in 1789.

"The ore is brought from (Anglesea) to be smelted at Swansea, and being formed into cakes and ingots, from three quarters to a hundredweight, is carried by the Severn trows to Brimscomb Port, on the Thames and Severn Canal, and then by flat-bottomed Thames barges along its course to the Mills. In time of war, the copper is manufactured chiefly into bolts and sheathings for ships, for the use of government. In peace, various kinds of sheet are formed for different domestic purposes, and for foreign trade. About fifty men and boys are employed in this establishment, which consists of a hammer mill, a bolt mill, and a flat-rolling mill, wholly worked by water. From 600 to 1,000 tons of copper are annually manufactured here. The men are paid by the great, or piece-work."

In 1848 T. Weedon and Sons started the manufacture of brown paper, the buildings being adapted and extended for the purpose and in 1861 there were no less than two hundred and fifty people employed here. There were four main water wheels and one high-water wheel operating at the turn of the century, driving paper-making machinery and water pumps. Their use was dimished about 1940 when they were adapted to drive electrical generators, which they continued to do for the next ten years. The framework of the two remaining wheels was inspected in 1972. One was made of cast iron, the other of oak, which could generate 100 h.p. and was said to be the largest on the Thames. Many types of cover papers were made here until about 1950 when other paper-based products including a new type of board combining paper and waste plastics was produced. The plant was finally wound up in 1969.

A little way down the river at Marlow there stood a large complex of weather-boarded mills which served the town and surrounding country-side for centuries but unfortunately little is known of their history. Corn milling was undoubtedly of paramount importance from the beginning of the growth of the medieval town and was still being carried out in the 20th century.

There was room at Marlow for several water wheels and a good head of water from a huge weir which provided sufficient power for industrial uses alongside the corn mill. From about 1700 John Lofting began the manufacture of thimbles on a large scale, and Daniel

Temple Mills 1973

Defoe speaks of two mills "both extraordinary in themselves, one for making of thimbles, a work excellently well finished, and which performs to admiration, and another for pressing of oyl from rapeseed . . . ." These two mills, one on either side of the corn mill, are shown on the plan of the estate of Mrs Elizabeth Ferrars which was produced in 1753. The plan also shows the great 'Ware', much longer than it is today, extending right down to the thimble mill. This was twenty years before the Thames Commissioners built the first pound lock by the mill and built up the island which lay just below the weir. Prior to this the barge traffic had to negotiate the flashlock in the middle of the weir with the aid of a capstan situated by Poor's Wharf at the bottom of St. Peter Street.

The industrial buildings were later used for the manufacture of paper. A plan of 1816 shows that a new building had been erected by paper millers Joseph and Edward Wright, replacing the thimble mill. A few years later they had also converted the old oil mill into a paper manufactory and now owned a large portion of the adjacent property. For a time they appear to have leased the first paper mill to a Mr. Pepper. The paper business prospered until at least 1899 under the name of William Wright and Sons. The water wheels ceased turning in 1941 but the buildings were not demolished until the 1950's to make way for a modern residential block.

The ancient weir at Marlow in 1753

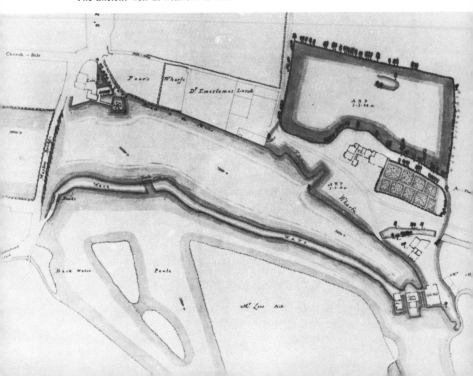

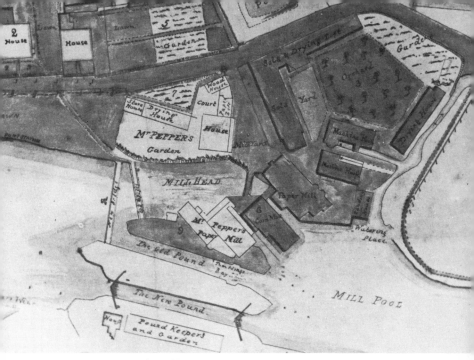

Plan of Marlow Paper Mills 1827

Cookham Manor has two mills recorded in Domesday. After Domesday the next references to a mill are in the first accounts of the Bailiff of Cookham and Bray, concerning goods sold by the manor from 1242-1247. The Bailiff, Godfrey de Lyston, gives account of the thirty-fourth year of the reign of Henry VIII and includes, "11 quarters of corn and 3 quarters and 2 bushels of malt of the issue of a certain mill bought this year sold". This appears to refer to a new mill recently built. The account of the following year includes 3 bushels of "Flowe".

In 1287-8 the costs of the mill refer to four pence for "iron and steel bought and placing on the bills of the mill". A mill bill being a tool shaped rather like a miniature pick, which was used for dressing the surfaces of the millstones. Iron was one of the few commodities which had to be imported from outside the manor and was also required for plough-shares and other implements.

In 1321-1322 John le Hen (or Ken), Keeper of the Kings Manor, rendered account of four pounds "of the farm of one watermill with fishery thereof so demised this year". Expenses included the stipend

71

Marlow Mills 1865

of one man, "for making three hundred piles of the lords timber and fixing the same in the wear (weir) of the mill; five shillings by the job". Accounts the following year include the cost of a further four hundred piles in the weir between the water of the Lord the King and the water of Walter le White and in lengthening the spindle of the mill and sharpening the bills. Walter le White resided at the Manor of Bullocks in Cookham, the present White Place Farm.

By 1379 the mill was "wholly broken down" and appears to have remained in ruins, for it is again mentioned as such a hundred years later in 1477. This old mill was referred to again in 1633 as being "since decayed". Therefore it was probably situated somewhere near the tail of modern Odney weir stream.

For several centuries the records do not mention a mill here although the millpond fishery is referred to many times. The few references to Ray Mills in Maidenhead during this period seem to indicate that they had taken over the industry now that the town was becoming economically and socially more important than its older neighbouring mother settlements.

A local fieldname in Cookham suggests that a windmill might have been built at one time, but no other record exists. It is more likely that the humble tenants of the scattered manor farms had to trudge up to two miles beside their cart or pack animal whenever corn was needed to be ground and take their turn behind the wealthier town tradesmen. "Raye Mills at Cookham" were certainly a going concern in 1346 when a lease transferred them from Nicholas atte Reye to Hugh of Berewyke (Braywick?). Other references occur in the 14th century and in 1510 when one mill was held with the Manor of Spencers by the well-known Norreys family. The corn mill was working here until the end of the last century. Around 1912 it was either burnt down or demolished.

What is today known as the Millstream at Cookham was originally the 'Lullebroc' mentioned as early as 1205, when King John gave Adam de Burnham a mill or fish dam and land in Cookham out of the Windsor Castle estate. In 1590 the Manor of Lulibrokes was conveyed by William Weldon to Thomas Turner. Except for the 1205 reference the stream never seems to be mentioned in connection with a mill or fishery, indeed the usually accurate Rocque Map of the mid-18th century does not appear to show it at all. There are several buried channels running across Formosa Island. It is possible that in company with these, old Lullibrook had silted up, but it could have been re-dug in the latter part of the 18th century for the new paper mill. However, this theory is jeopardised by A.H. Shorters' reference to a paper mill or miller at Cookham in 1658, but unfortunately no source is given. In the Bucks Session Records of about 1700, Joseph Darvall is named as Cookham Miller but he was already leasing Taplow Mill and therefore may have only resided at Cookham.

In 1719 a certain William Fennable was renting property from a High Wycombe paper maker. This could be the William Venables who about forty years later started manufacturing "Whitey" or whited brown paper at premises in Cookham on the site of the present mill house, premises which were probably leased to him, as in 1797 they were insured by Cook, a Rickmansworth papermaker. The paper mill was later in the Venables family until 1893, when it finally ceased operating and was rebuilt as a private residence.

The Venables family was very well known in the area at one time, as they also had the paper mill at Taplow. This was probably started by William's son in the late 18th century and founded upon a very ancient mill site, for in 1194 two water mills were included in the estates of Amerden Manor in Taplow held by William Turville who had leased them from the Priory of Merton. In 1304 three mills are mentioned. In 1315 Merton Priory leased to John the Dyer, a fulling mill and two islands for forty shillings a year, which his father had held before him. The Cookham accounts of 1465 include a new rent of sixpence for "one island of half an acre on the east side between Tappeslow Myll and the bridge of Maidenhith".

In 1551 the Prior of Merton demised the Manor to Thomas Manfield but retained the Mills (in 1573 Henry Manfield's lands included Cliveden Park and Pages Wharf below Hedsor). In 1613 an attempt was made to set up an overshot mill at Taplow but this apparently was not a success, probably because it would have ruined the other mills by using an excessive head of water.

Previously, in 1523, the fulling mill had been demised to John Holderness (probably the same Holderness who held a weir on the Cookham fisheries) for twenty years at eight pounds ten shillings. In 1544 Jane, probably his widow, renewed the lease. Again in 1562 Queen Elizabeth demised "The Milne of Taplow and Baye and islands to the said mill, Teynteryt, Assheyte, Glasmaiseye and Normans eyte" to Jane and her son Roger, at the same time passing the property to the Honour of Windsor. Roger undertook to repair the mill, which was then ruinous, and was granted a further lease in 1580.

In 1605 Sir Henry Guildford held the mills with the Manor, but this soon passed to the Hampson family, Thomas being created a baronet in 1642. About 1700 the Manor was transferred to the Earl of Orkney. The fishery depositions of 1633 had described the mills as "two corn milles under one roof, anciently called Clevedon Mills, from an ancient owner called William of Cleveden". In 1696 a sale of rents of Windsor Castle included a rent out of Taplow Mills of eleven pounds among other local free farm rents conveyed to the Earl of Portland. In 1698 a corn mill was leased to one Joseph Darvell for sixty pounds a year. Joseph was probably the father of Peter Darvill, Bargemaster of Maidenhead, who was threatened for running his barges through the Reading "Blockade" on the Kennet in 1725. Three mills were working throughout the 18th century, including in the latter half Venables' successful paper making concern which still flourishes as the New Taplow Paper Mills.

For thousands of years the Thames has been eroding the cliff face of Cliveden, especially at the top end of the reach where the chalk wall receives the full brunt of the current on the great bend underneath Hedsor. Several hundred feet of chalk once stood where Cookham Church now stands. Slowly it gave way before the undercutting river, leaving behind the accumulated alluviums which are Odney and Sashes and the several ancient channels between them. One of the contributory factors which helped the erosion of the chalk, was the small river, variously called the Wycombe Stream, Wick, Wyk or Wye, which runs roughly south from West Wycombe, down the steep-sided Wycombe Valley into the Thames at Bourne End. It is possible that at one time the course of the river took it into the Thames lower down because a small stream called Blessings Ditch runs from springs near Hedsor Village and joins the main river on the bend at Hedsor Wharf. This could be a remnant of the Wye which was possibly diverted in the Middle Ages and which now skirts the modern western boundary of Hedsor Parish.

In 1492 this tiny manor is described as having two mills. Earlier, in 1360, two weirs were mentioned. In 1541 we have a Hedsor Mill and in 1556 two water mills are included in a sale of the wharves and lands of Sir Edmund Peckham. In 1632 the Water Poet, John Taylor, says of Hedsor "... a spring runs from the chalkie hills, which not long ago did turn two mills" which seems to indicate Blessings Ditch as being the mill stream, indeed the so-called Pile Dwellings found near the stream's confluence with the Thames may be nothing more than part of an old mill dam or weir. On the other hand the Hedsor mill site may have always been on the River Wye at Bourne End. Robert Lunnon was a paper and pasteboard maker here in 1770 and the family business flourished throughout the 19th century. Apart from the paper and pasteboard mill, another waterwheel served a corn mill which stood on the opposite bank of the stream. The mills were given to two sons, and to avoid arguments over possible water shortages their father stipulated that if necessary the corn mill could be used for nine hours per day, from 6 a.m. to 3 p.m. From then on the sluice gate could be raised to start turning the wheel which drove the paper-making machinery. During the 1914-18 war waste paper was brought by barge to the Townsend Wharf at Bourne End. Messrs Jackson bought the paper and board mill around 1917 but the Lunnon family were still very much in evidence in the area with their farming interests, which include the ancient abbey farm at Little Marlow.

The Romans found the winding and sheltered Wycombe Valley to be a pleasant habitat, as did many prehistoric peoples before them, but the sparkling River Wye had to await the Saxon settlers before it could begin its long career as one of the most industrious little rivers in southern England. Shallow draughted boats were soon creeping up the main river laden with huge millstones imported from a distance, for you cannot grind corn with chalk or gravel.

By 1086 there were no less than eight mills operating in Wooburn Manor and the steep trackways leading to the hilltop farms began to deepen under the hooves of heavily laden animals bringing produce to the valley. For hundreds of years the river served the small sheltered agricultural communities on its banks, providing flour, fish and fowl. But suddenly, early in the 17th century, paper-making came to South Bucks and the clean and pure river, being highly suited to this purpose, was rapidly turned into the factory tool and waste disposal drain we know today.

Paper-making was introduced into England in the 16th century. In 1597 John Spilman, Queen Elizabeth's jeweller, was given sole rights of manufacture, but four years later wrote complaining that John Turner, Edward Marshall and George Ffrend had erected a mill in Buckinghamshire and were collecting the finest rags and material for making paper. By the 1620s mills were said to be operating on the Wye and Colne rivers, corn mills were being converted to paper-making and sometimes the two industries existed side by side under the same roof. The early industrialists who came to the valley were not exactly welcomed with open arms, incurring stiff opposition from the start because they brought in skilled workers and their families from elsewhere.

In 1635-6, during an epidemic of the plague, the selling of London rags for paper-making spread the infection into the countryside and the mills were ordered to stop production. Paper-makers successfully claimed compensation and an extra rate, or tax, was imposed for the relief of the paper workers and their families who had so recently been brought into the parishes. Thus the indigenous population incurred a bitter financial burden on top of that already brought by the plague. A petition from the angry locals to the Commissioners of the Peace for Buckinghamshire and Middlesex gave as many reasons as possible why paper-makers and their kind should be banished off the face of the earth.

"We under favour doe conceive that the said milles be utterley suppressed . . . for in the last great Plague before this, and this year also, the infection has been brought into these places by the means of their ragges, as to Colebrooke, Horton, Wickcomb and Woborne . . . they fetch ragges also from places beyounde the seas where att those times the plague hath been, by which meanes we are in perpetuall feare. The grounds and highwayes adjoining to these milles have been much anoyed by the high penning up of the waters farr above the size whereas the sayde grounds killed and the sayd wayes rather become passages for boates than highwayes for men and horses to travile. The fishes in the river have been and are dayly destroyed and hindered from striving upp by reason of the double wheels of the sayd milles running neare to the bottom, to the depth of an inch and a half with great violence, and allowances which should allways be open for the passage of ffishes are made soe narrow and layde soe hygh as the ffishes can by noe meanes passe. And basketts and clothes are layd to catch the sayd ffishes in their strivings and the said allowances are stopped to procure more water to their sayd milles. The bordering inhabitants are much anoyed by the hideous noyse of the hammers of the paper mills which goe daye and night without intermission even on Sundayes, which are heard two or three miles off".

The petition goes on to say that the corn markets are much decayed as many mills have been converted to paper making and the corn mills in existence not worked properly, also the inhabitants are afraid to go to the mills because of the plague risk. Lastly, paper-makers were said to be of great annoyance to the country in general because even though they first made good paper, it is now "soe unuseful as will bear no incke on any side" and had become very expensive.

Local antagonism was not all that paper-makers and millers in general had to put up with, there was always the risk of fire. A few insurance companies did exist but few millers could afford the premiums which were doubled for wooden buildings. Therefore in about the year 1700 poor William Church of Wooburn, his wife and seven children, found themselves totally destitute following a dreadful fire which destroyed his house and mills. The Bucks quarter sessions of 1717 included a deposition regarding another fire, this time at Loudwater, higher up the valley at the mill of Jeremiah Francis, a leading English paper maker. It gives some idea of the number and type of buildings on a mill site at this time and the finances involved.

"Jeremiah Francis of Loudewater in the Parish of Chepping Wycombe, paper maker, and many witnesses testified to a sudden and dreadful fire breaking out in the paper warehouse or drying rooms adjoining his paper mills, which in a short time burnt down the said paper mills, the water-corn mills, the mill house wherein the said Jeremiah Francis lived, the adjoining outhouses, warehouses, buildings, barns and stables and a great quantity of paper and materials for making paper, all the implements, tools and utensils that were used in the making of paper and grinding of corn in the said mills and many of his household goods, and other goods, chattels and wares. Upon the examination of William Turner, millwright, David Beckford, carpenter, Richard Seare, bricklayer, and Henry Blackwell, papermaker, able and experienced workmen, the loss sustained by the said Jeremiah Francis in the paper mills, water cornmills, millhouses, outhouses, buildings, barns, warehouses and shops amounted to £321 16s. 0d. and on the paper, material for making paper, grinding corn and his household goods, hay, wood, corn, grain and other goods and chattels, the sum of £146 0s. 4d."

Hedsor Mills c. 1900

Francis was granted Letters Patent to collect charitable benevolence for his loss, as he was now totally impoverished.

In 1724 Defoe describes the Wye as having "a great many mills, and particularly corn mills and paper mills; the first of these grind and dress the wheat, and then the wheat is sent to Marlow..." (More likely to Bourne End or Hedsor Wharf) "and loaded on board the barges for London. And the second makes great quantities of printing paper, and that very good of its kind, and cheap, such as generally is made use of in printing our newspapers, journals etc, and smaller pamphlets; but not much fine, or large, for bound books, or writing".

So despite early opposition, the Wye Valley had rapidly become one of the main centres of paper manufacture in the country. In 1690 the Mayor of Chepping Wycombe could claim that there were already eight paper mills in the parish employing fifty families. Here the product was mainly good quality white paper, but further down the river where the water had become less pure, brown paper and paper board were produced. There was a board mill at Bourne End as early as 1719, and several more in the area by the end of the century, including Lunnon's at Hedsor, Revells at Eghams Green and Thomas and Sarah Wildmans' at the confluence of the Wye and Thames at Bourne End.

At the early part of the 19th century there were about five hundred paper mills in the country, the greatest density being in South Bucks, especially on the Wye, where there were over thirty. Early paper was made in a tedious and painstaking way, one sheet at a time, and many people were employed for each process in the production. So we come to one of the many incidents typical of the industrial revolution, when in 1830 many skilled papermakers met under the cherry trees on Flackwell Heath and then proceeded down the valley, besieging the mills and smashing the new-fangled paper-making machines which threatened their jobs. The machines stayed but the number of mills drastically declined, and those that remain to this day have grown into great complexes providing work for hundreds of people.

4 · ROADS AND BRIDGES

To illustrate the past economic and social importance of river transport, not only on the Thames but on navigable waterways throughout Britain, we must take a look at the road system, or rather the lack of it, that prevailed up to the 19th century.

It is doubtful if the early Saxon settlers used the crumbling legacy of Roman roads to any great degree. They founded their villages, farmed their own small fields and sat tight. The wandering Danes, once the fighting was done, were also content to hold the small pieces of land they had wrested from the earlier settlers. Up to and including the time of the Norman Conquest the only long distance travellers were the missionaries and the fighting bands, travelling on foot or on horseback and living off the country.

With the later growth of castles, towns and the large farming estates of the monasteries, rough tracks developed, leading from the countryside to fairs and markets, and from town to town. Wide drove roads also developed as livestock was taken to the main centres of population, especially London. In the Court Rolls as late as 1824 there is a complaint that the valuable grazing on Maidenhead Moor had been damaged by droves of sheep on their way to London. Most highways were no more than rights of way established through long usage and kept in reasonable condition by the lord, or rather his tenants. Up to the time of the Dissolution, the monasteries kept a watchful eye on the upkeep of the highways, especially those which were economically important to themselves. But upkeep meant only that they filled in the worst of the pot-holes and occasionally trimmed back the encroaching forest. In 1285 Edward I decreed that in order to forestall robbers, all trees and undergrowths were to be cut back to a distance of two hundred feet on either side of the King's Highway, but like many other laws of the time it was not effectively enforced.

Throughout the Middle Ages practically the only wheeled transport was the harvest cart or tumbril, suitable for local work around

81

Road versus River in 1847

the farm or village. Because the highways remained mere tracks, the long distance carriage of goods was undertaken by strings of pack horses, mules and asses. Large numbers of these animals, up to forty in a string, were still to be seen in the hilly regions of the country such as Devon and Cornwall in the 19th century.

Four-wheeled stage wagons were introduced at some time in the 16th century and rapidly increased in numbers. At first they were capable of carrying only a couple of tons but by the 18th century loads had increased to eight tons, hauled by up to twelve draught oxen or horses. Besides carrying goods of all sorts, these vast lumbering covered wagons were the only means of transport for young or infirm travellers going from place to place; the healthy poor walked, the rich rode on horseback.

The stage wagons caused extensive damage to the existing tracks, most of which were no more than bridleways. Early attempts were made to improve the system, as in 1555 when it was enacted that village constables and church wardens could order householders to contribute material or labour for road repairs or otherwise pay a fine. Unpaid surveyors were appointed, who naturally looked after their own interests. A statement by one named Harrison, in the reign of Elizabeth I, sums up the usefulness of the early acts.

82

"All sorts of the common people are employed for six days in summer for repairs but the rich doo so cancell their portions and the poor so loiter in their labour that scarcely two good days labour are performed in a parish." Instead of repairing roads from market to market, surveyors did work on roads leading to their own fields. This six day system continued into the 17th century.

The average speed of land journeys was no more than about ten miles a day in winter, if you were lucky, and not much more in summer. Travellers on horseback did not have much of an advantage over the slower wagons, which churned the track into an impassable morass in winter and left deep wheel ruts in other seasons. This sometimes left a high and narrow causeway between the ruts on which the travellers on horseback rode. On approaching one another it was quite usual for riders, being unable to pass, to sit for hours until one rider lost patience and dared his horse to attempt to negotiate the broken ground to the side. To deviate too much from the known highway was to be lost in a wild inhospitable countryside where a stranger was looked upon with hostility.

In about 1592 two Dukes of Wirtemburg described their journey along the Oxford road. "We passed through a villianous, boggy and wild country, and several times missed our way, because the country thereabouts is very little inhabited, and is nearly a waste; and there is one spot in particular where the mud is so deep that in my opinion it would be scarcely possible to pass with a coach in winter or in rainy weather". In 1624, one of the reasons for the Act to improve the Thames navigation between Burcot and Oxford was that "the said passage will be very behoveful for preserving the highways leading to and from the said university and city and other parts thereabouts", which owing to the continuous passage of carts had become dangerous for travellers in winter "and hardly to be amended or continued passable without exceeding charge".

All road transport was often frozen into a state of immobility during bad winters, but when conditions allowed, carriers operated over considerable distances and by the middle of the 17th century there was regular, albeit slow service along all the major roads of England. Light passenger coaches gradually evolved alongside the goods wagons. In April 1669 the first 'flying' coach managed to stagger from London to Oxford in one day, and the coaching era had begun. As early as 1673 there were complaints that coaches were running to and from London and every little town in the Thames Valley up as far as Maidenhead, carrying passengers, letters and packets previously carried by water.

Sunken road from Cookham to Marlow. Quarry Woods 1974

The weight of the monstrous stage wagons and the numbers of great draught animals required to pull them, dug deep into the highways. Wagoners would deviate from obstructions and larger potholes so that the major highways grew outwards until they could be up to one hundred yards wide and looked more like drift roads. In the 18th century there were several attempts to stop the erosion by the wagons. Broad wheels were made compulsory; at first a width of nine inches was tried, and then sixteen inches. Wagoners were encouraged by the turnpike trustees to fit wider wheels.

84

The Craftsman 1875

Generally, conditions in the two centuries before the improvements of Telford and MacAdam and the Turnpike Trusts in the mid-18th century, and in some places for long afterwards, were probably worse for travel than they were in medieval times. This was not only due to the increasing traffic, but lack of organised maintenance since the fall of the monastic system, coupled with a lack of funds for internal development during the long and expensive wars.

For transportation of goods in bulk, water transport was still supreme. There were many complaints about barges being held up for long periods during droughts, especially during the frantic profit race of the industrial revolution, but road traffic was also delayed for long spells in winter often being snow-bound for weeks. Generally the travelling speed did not vary much whether by land or water, but the loads that could be carried or pulled by one horse varied enormously. A packhorse carried about one eighth of a ton, one draught horse could pull five eighths of a ton on 'soft' roads and two tons on MacAdamed roads. But one horse towing a barge on a river could pull an average of thirty tons and on a canal, fifty tons. The cost of land carriage in the 18th century was at least three times greater than that by water, and where bulk cargoes such as coal were concerned, the ratio was much greater. This situation continued until there was a dramatic change of fortunes with the coming of the railways in the mid-19th century.

The histories of road and river meet at two main points; at wharves and bridges. Of the old town and village wharves few traces remain; a quay wall and an ancient warehouse utilised by a boat-

Scene at Windsor Bridge 1793

yard is all that may be left of a once thriving inland port. Perhaps there is only a street name; in no instance are the remains spectacular, or even pleasing to the eye. Bridges on the other hand, at least in the majority of cases, have a special kind of sanctity and beauty, and are often the only remaining sign that history touched the river at all. Few traces remain of the other earlier means of river crossing, by ford or ferry, although the past importance of fording is commemorated in many place-names.

The line of communication had to be of major importance for the

difficult and costly construction of a bridge to be even considered. In common with many early roads, bridges were founded and maintained by the local religious establishment for communication and trade. Towns, especially after the Dissolution of the Monasteries, also formed religious guilds to maintain their own structures. A chapel was usually placed on or near the bridge and kept by a priest or hermit; here travellers were persuaded to offer gifts which in theory went towards the upkeep of the bridge. Parcels of land went with the chapel, the profits of which were for the same purpose. However, after the priest's living had been subtracted there was usually very little money left for repairs. Most money came from pontage and pavage (under and over) tolls, for the collection of which the authority in charge appointed wardens and clerks. Tolls were charged on road and river transport alike, and on the merchandise carried. Sometimes charges were made for only a term of years, especially when a bridge needed extensive repairs or rebuilding.

Most of the Saxon and Norman bridges were made of wood, a material which rotted and broke up in a comparatively short time, especially at the water line, and timbers had to be frequently replaced. Even so, wooden bridges were used on major routes for many centuries until the heavy road transport of the industrial revolution required stronger structures in stone and iron. Amongst those of the middle and lower Thames, Caversham bridge existed as a strange half timber, half stone or brick structure until the 1850s, and they were completely made of timber at Henley, Marlow, Cookham, Maidenhead, Windsor, Staines, Chertsey, Hampton and Kingston.

Wooden bridges were simply constructed as horizontal or slightly curved plank roadways, perched on rows of closely set piles which were driven deep into the riverbed. The rows of piles were usually placed fairly close together across the river to provide as much strength as possible, but on all bridges there were one or two much wider gaps for the barge traffic to pass through. This explains why wooden bridges continued to be used from the medieval period onwards on the busier reaches, for apart from the dearth of the other building materials of brick and stone in those areas, there was not the technical knowledge available to build stone archways of a sufficient span and headroom to allow the passage of large craft encumbered with high loads. In any case, the massive piers and abutments that would have then been required to support the weight of stone would have seriously restricted the flow of water between them, which of course was the case with old London Bridge. The beautiful old bridges of the upper Thames, mostly dating from the 12th to the 15th centuries, were built of stone, primarily because it was available locally and because the restricted arches could easily accommodate the smaller craft which used the shallow reaches.

From Marlow to Maidenhead we have a cross section of Thames bridges, the histories of which are fairly typical of the majority. The first Marlow bridge has been attributed to the Knights Templars who held lands in Bisham, on the Berkshire bank. This bridge was already ancient and apparently in a bad state of repair as early as the beginning of the 14th century, for in 1309 there was granted a pontage of one penny for four years on all barges carrying merchandise valued at over forty shillings to go towards urgent maintenance. Throughout the 14th century and probably until the Dissolution the bridge was in the charge of the Abbey of Bisham. In 1565 John Seymour left "one convenient oak" per year for 60 years for maintenance.

During the Civil War it suffered the fate of many others up and down the river, being partly destroyed by the parliamentary forces. After repairs it lasted on this first site (probably on the line of the present bridge) until 1789 when a new wooden bridge was built slightly lower down abutting St. Peter Street, the old Duck Lane. The cost was £1800, raised by public subscription chiefly with the help of

The Conventual Barn of Bisham Abbey by Marlow Bridge 1870

Cookham Ferry 1834

George, Marquis of Buckingham. In 1792 Ireland says "It has a remarkable ascent, and forms the best object as a wooden bridge, that I
remember to have seen. The ballustrades are painted white, in imita-
tion of stonework. . ."

In 1835 the wood was at last replaced with the 217 foot span of the
iron suspension bridge by Tierney Clark, initially costing £22,000,
and this has lasted to the present day. In 1972 the gleaming new concrete bridge of the Marlow and Bisham Bypass took some of the
weight off the ancient ironwork, and with luck it will be preserved for
many years to come.

Just upstream from the bridge on the Marlow shore there once
stood a venerable building called the Conventual Barn of Bisham
Abbey. Undoubtably medieval in origin it may have served as a warehouse for market produce to and from the Abbey Estates and the
town. During the 19th century it held French prisoners of war and
then served as a coal depot. Luckily it was drawn and photographed

Cookham Ferry and Timber Bridge 1865

on several occasions prior to its demolition in 1878 when many of the roof timbers went into the building of Lane End Church nearby. The ancient foundations of chalk and flint were exposed recently, prior to the erection of a new housing block.

The iron railway bridge at Bourne End was constructed in the 1890's replacing an earlier wooden bridge of 1854. It serves the branch line which originally went from Maidenhead to High Wycombe but which now terminates at Bourne End, with the link to Marlow.

There was no bridge at Cookham until the 19th century. Until then a ferry was all that was required to serve the needs of the small farming communities in the two counties on either side of the river. Cookham Ferry was of importance from an early period. This is confirmed by the large amount of medieval pottery which litters a nearby riverside garden, and by 14th century references in Ministers' accounts when it was included in fishery rents to the Crown.

At the "Court of Fairs" in 1470 the jury presented that the Abbot of Cirencester permitted the ferry barge "to be ruinous whereby the people cannot cross". Another complaint came in 1591 when Mr.

Cockham Toll Bridge 1947

Manfield (presumably of Cliveden), Francis Edward James and John Browne "bar'd the passage of Cookham divers times with their boats, where of right they ought not to use, to the great hurt of the inhabitants...." In the 17th century the ferry was leased with other property in Cookham including the Malthouse and a ferry cottage formerly occupied by Hugh Cottrell, a local fisherman.

By 1840, when the first wooden bridge was built by Freebody, the ferry had become a lucrative business, for it cost the Bridge Company £2565 to buy it. The materials and construction of this first bridge came to £4224, and the Authorising Act and other costs came to £1485.

This first bridge was practically collapsing only twenty years later but may have soldiered on until 1870 when the new bridge, the present uninspired iron structure was completed. Tolls ceased here in

92

1947 but the octagonal brick Toll House remains. Until the great increase in motor transport Cookham remained a country bridge, used by the local shepherd when driving his flocks to Wycombe Market, and by the mill workers cycling to shift work at Bourne End through the early morning mist. They used to lead the toll collector a dance, each one in the line telling him that the one behind was going to pay his penny, until no one did.

Maidenhead bridge is situated on the major route out of London to the West Country, therefore the site is of great antiquity. An early timber bridge was almost in ruins in 1297. In 1337 there was pontage of one penny on all laden vessels passing through, and in 1376 the watermen were complaining of a similar charge. At the beginning of the 15th century repairs were carried out under the supervision of the Prior of Bisham, who already had a considerable amount of bridge building experience from his other responsibility at Marlow.

At the beginning of the reign of Henry IV there was a plot to restore the deposed King Richard II. On the first Sunday of the year 1400, the Duke of Exeter, the Duke of Surrey and the Earl of Salisbury met at Kingston with 8,000 archers and 300 lances of Men at Arms, sending a letter to the young Earl of Rutland in London to join them in the attack on the King at Windsor.

Rutland however, was forced to turn traitor. King Henry escaped

Maidenhead Bridge Tollgate c. 1900

to London, quickly raised a force of 16,000 men and advanced along the Great West Road towards the insurgent forces who made a rapid retreat over Maidenhead Bridge. The rebel rearguard under the command of the Duke of Surrey, held the bridge for a considerable time against the vanguard of King Henry's army, whilst the main part of the rebel force retreated through Henley towards Oxford.

One who lost his head for complicity in the abortive rebellion was Sir Bernard Brocas, whose estates, including the manors of Cookham and Bray, were escheated to the Crown. However, the following year the lands were handed back to William, the eldest son, and the widow Johanna.

In 1452 a charter of Henry VI placed the fraternity under the supervision of the Chauntry Priest, Thomas Mettyngham. He had complained that "divers lieges of the King cannot cross without peril at certain times of the year through floods and the weakness of the bridge". He was granted leave to acquire lands to the value of ten marks for repairs and pontage "for ever", and lands and water for fifty feet on either side. A weekly market, on Wednesdays, was also granted, and a toll charged on all merchandise sold.

In 1530 Leland mentions the thriving timber wharf at the bridge. After the Reformation the town was incorporated anew as the "Wardens and Burgesses" of Maidenhead. James II granted another charter of incorporation with the style of Mayor, Bridge Masters and Burgesses. It appears that the upkeep of the bridge was so

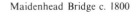

Maidenhead Bridge c. 1800

important that each reigning monarch went to great lengths to keep on good terms with the town, so that the road remained open.

In 1688 the old bridge was fortified to impede the progress of the Prince of Orange towards London, the defence being entrusted to a Irish contingent. But on one dark night some of the townsmen came towards the barricades beating a Dutch march, so scaring the Irish that they took to their heels, leaving their cannon behind them.

In 1772 an Act was passed authorising the construction of a new bridge. "Whereas the said timber bridge is narrow and incommodious and so greatly decayed, that in the opinion of able and experienced workmen it ought to be taken down and a new bridge built". This was designed in Portland stone by the famous architect Sir Robert Taylor, whose other commissions included additions to the Bank of England and riverside landmarks such as Harleyford Manor House, Wallingford Church, possibly Swinford Toll Bridge at Eynsham and alterations to Old London Bridge in 1760. The new Maidenhead Bridge was built about fifty yards below the old one and was opened in 1777. The contractor was John Townesend of Oxford. Two single storied toll houses lay at the Maidenhead end.

Exempted from tolls were cattle drawing carts loaded with dung or hay, to be laid up within 2 miles, cattle drawing coaches with passengers, passengers on horseback going to or from elections, post horses or carts with mail, army personnel and carriages carrying vagrants sent by passes.

Tolls were collected until 1903 when one riotous day the inhabitants of the town, with great glee, hurled the gates into the river, from whence they had to be recovered by the Council workmen. The bridge estates formerly included land on either bank and four properties in Maidenhead High Street, including Number 16, the Church Gate House.

The bridge is still structurally sound, and has recently received a well-deserved facelift, for it is one of the area's finest ancient monuments. The traditional postcard view may be marred in the next few years by the construction of a new single spanned concrete bridge on the upstream side built to cope with increasing traffic congestion. So the original structure will be well and truly hemmed in, for on the down-stream side there sits Brunel's solid monument of the railway age, the 'Sounding Arch', the largest brick built span in Europe.

5 · NAVIGATION IN
THE 17th CENTURY

In 1605 "Boates and barges of great content and carriage" were trading regularly up and down the river from London to within a few miles of Oxford. At Burcot on the Wittenham loop above Dorchester the heaviest goods had to be unloaded and transferred to wagons for the last few creaking miles by road to the city. Lighter cargoes were transferred to shallower draughted vessels which could navigate up to Oxford and beyond. Deeply laden vessels were not able to proceed much further than Burcot, especially during low water conditions, because of the rock bed at Clifton Hampden and the extensive shallows below Oxford.

The poor condition of the main route for trade out of Oxford was a thorn in the side of the merchants, and so in 1607 the so-called Oxford to Burcot Commissioners met to discuss what they could do about it. The Commission included men of the City and University and the important land owners in the surrounding counties. Apart from ordering a quantity of timber which should have been used for river improvement but eventually went to Sir Thomas Bodley's library, they did very little until the river improvement act of 1624 forced them into action. No doubt the act was prompted by the demand for Cotswold stone from the Oxfordshire quarries but there was also an increasing demand in Oxford for sea coal and other necessities from London. Another factor was that the carriage of heavy goods by wagon had made the Oxfordshire roads almost impassable in winter. The 1624 act authorised the building of three pound locks below Oxford, at Iffley and Sandford Mills and on the Swift Ditch, an ancient channel of the Thames which by-passes Abingdon around Andersey Island.

A lock is an extremely simple device, but its importance must not be underestimated. It is as important to inland water transport as the wheel is to land transport. Its use on British canals was one of the most vital links in the chain which led to the industrial revolution, for good or evil it changed the face of the world.

Summer outing at Cookham Lock c. 1890

All rivers naturally have a downward slope or gradient from the source to the sea; the bed of the river falls with the fall of the land, the surface of the water also has a similar gradient. The Thames has sufficient flow of water for the greater part of the year for it to be navigable at least as far as Oxford without the aid of weirs and locks, or rather it would have if the gradient was constant. In practice however, the gradient varies with the lie of the land, depending on geological variations such as chalk outcrops or nicks in the valley left by ancient shorelines. Therefore we get bumps and levelling off of the river bed while the water surface remains level in comparison, leading to some parts of the river being shallower than others. Therefore some method had to be devised to carry deep draughted barges over the shallows. Firstly, of course, we had the flash-locks built into the mill dams which were situated on the chalk outcrops where there were usually convenient islands. By this method the river was made into a flattened but gigantic flowing staircase, each step several miles long being raised or lowered to match the height of the next step at

97

either end by the use of a flush of water. As we have seen, this was extremely wasteful and inconvenient for all concerned. However, long ago some unknown genius had already discovered that craft could be raised and lowered to different levels by floating them into a chamber of water not much longer than the craft itself.

Canals linking navigable rivers were being built in China as far back as 200 B.C., using single stop-log gates on the flashlock principle for changes in levels. The best known of these is the Grand Canal to Peking, which by the 13th century was 700 miles long. It is likely that at an early date stop-log gates were being placed close together, making the first pound locks. It was not until the 14th century that the idea appeared in Europe, when large basins connecting Dutch rivers with canals incorporated two sets of port-cullis gates. In the following century pound locks with portcullis type gates were built by Bertola on several canals leading to Milan, but the credit for the invention of the pound lock incorporating Mitre gates with built-in vertical sluices goes to Leonardo da Vinci, who sketched out the design of the lock as we know it today for the San Marco Lock on the Naviglio Interno, Milan, in 1495.

The modern lock consists of a chamber with vertical walls (usually parallel to each other but the shapes have varied over the centuries, and there have even been circular basins) with a pair of solid wooden gates at either end. The heel post of each gate is held by a metal strap to the top of the lock wall and by a socket in the river bed in which it pivots. As a gate closes it butts up against its partner and at the same time comes up against a cill at the bottom of the river, set in the form of a shallow 'V', the point of the 'V' facing upstream. In the same way that a pointed arch can withstand enormous pressures from above, mitre gates can hold back thousands of tons of water pressing against them and not collapse inwards. Yet when the water level is equal on both sides they may be opened with minimal force.

The upper gate cill is set at the depth of the upper section of the river or canal so that there is then a drop down on to the floor of the chamber, the depth of which depends on the height of the 'step' to be surmounted. The tail, or downstream cill and therefore of course the base of the tail gates, will be correspondingly lower. The cills are usually at a depth slightly exceeding the deepest draughted vessel expected. To fill and empty the chamber, water is let in and out through apertures in the base of the gates by the raising or lowering of sluice gates or paddles worked by various means. Some locks, especially on the canals, have ground sluices or tunnels in the lock walls, again worked by paddles.

Remains of Marlow Flashlock 1875

The first pound locks in England were built in 1564-7 for the lateral canal alongside the River Exe, making navigation possible from Exeter to the sea. These locks had mitre gates at the head and a single gate at the tail. A few years later (1571-4) the River Lea was improved at Waltham Abbey with the help of a pound lock with two sets of mitre gates. The first Thames turnpikes as they were then called, at Iffley, Sandford and Swift Ditch, were open for traffic by 1635. The original structures appear to have been built with timber walls which soon deteriorated, for in 1651 the wall of Swift Ditch collapsed and freestone was brought from Kennington to build a stronger lock. Iffley and Sandford were also rebuilt in stone, on

99

several occasions through the centuries, and the remains may be seen alongside their modern counterparts. Swift Ditch Lock has a different history because the navigation channel later reverted to the old Abingdon stream when the 18th century series of locks was built.

To see the tiny Swift Ditch today it is difficult to visualize that huge barges once passed to and fro along its winding course, but the fact that they did is proved by the gateless masonry walls of the old lock, which for over three hundred years have stood in their leafy setting at the upper end of the stream. This old lock could never have been a great success because of the silting up of the channel below it. Each time a lock is filled and emptied a certain amount of silt and gravel is drawn through, which tends to build up a shoal below the lock. The lesson was learnt by the engineers because later locks were sited at the lower end of lock cuts so that debris was discharged into the main river where there is less chance of shoaling.

At the time when the first Thames locks were under construction a certain John Taylor took a trip on the river. Taylor (1580-1653) was a well known Thames wherryman, poet, pamphleteer and traveller, much concerned with river improvements. His description in "Thames Isis" (1643) quoted by Thacker, includes:

". . . Then Marlow Lock is worse, I must confess
the water is so pinched with shallowness.
Beneath which is a weare should be defaced
and Cottrells weare of Cookham be displaced
A weare to one Holdernesse belong
Which doth the river most injourious wrong
Near which a spring runs from the chalkie hills
Which not long ago did turn two mills.
A stop against Taplow Warren doth much spread
Next Boulters Lock, (a mile from Maidenhead)."

Five years later he supplied another valuable description of river trade in his Carriers Cosmography: "To Bull Wharfe (near Queenhithe) there doe come and go great boats twice or thrice every week betwixt London and Kingston, great boats that doe carry passengers and goods betwixt London and Maydenhead, doe come every Munday and Thursday and goe away upon Tuesdays and Thursdays. The Reading boat is to be had at Queenhithe weekly".

A certain amount of barge traffic continued throughout the Civil War despite the obstructions of demolished bridges and locks. The

100

The old Flashlock at Boulters 1865

Royalists controlled much of the river in the early days, provisions and munitions getting through to the garrisons at Reading and Oxford. The voyages must have been fraught with danger from attack by Parliamentary skirmishers, and a bargeman's lot could not have been a happy one at the time. Even less happy was the lot of four barge loads of Scots prisoners, who in 1648 were taken down river from an overcrowded Windsor Castle to Gravesend to await transportation.

The bargeman's life was not much easier in 1650 when an act of the Puritan Parliament forbade the movement of all river traffic on Sundays. Troops stationed along the rivers enforced the ban. One can imagine the chagrin of a bargemaster with a perishable cargo having to lose twenty-four hours travelling time and perhaps a good flush of water into the bargain, and having to lie aground for several days. The Commonwealth Acts fell with the Restoration but the Sunday ban was re-enacted and not repealed until 1827 though not strictly enforced, although in 1710 Thomas Cocke of Fifield in Berkshire was arrested by the Hambleden Constable for the offence and indicted and fined 6s. 8d. after escaping from custody.

The second half of the 17th century brings many references to

101

Hayboats at Windsor 1812

'Western Barges' going from London to Oxford almost daily with provisions of all kinds and returning with West Country and Chiltern timber for the building of merchant and fighting ships and from all the riverside towns came vast quantities of another very important commodity, malt. After the great fire in 1666, Cotswold stone went to help in the rebuilding of London, including St. Pauls Cathedral. Passenger traffic on the lower river was in its heyday. There were ten thousand small boats between the Fleet river and Windsor. Wherries were rowed by members of that tough company of watermen as far as Maidenhead. The sleek wherry was a far more comfortable and cheaper means of transport than the first cumbersome coaches which were making an appearance, although they were somewhat slower, being "a sort of pleasure boat, at one end of which is a little room handsomely painted and covered, with a table in the middle and benches round it".

Bridges were few and far between so all along the river people used ferry boats, sometimes with tragic consequences. On one day in September 1594 six men, including a Mr. Goodluck, were drowned at Datchet Ferry, and in 1674 a broadsheet brought to Londoners "Sad and deplorable news from Oxfordsheir and Barksheir, being a true and lamentable relation of the drowning of about sixty persons, men, women, and children, in the lock near Goring in Oxfordsheir, as they were passing by water from Goring feast to Stately (Streatley) in Barksheir". The dangers are well known, and the river is respected, especially by the bankside residents, but year after year throughout the centuries it claims its victims.

In the late 17th century the state of the river for barge traffic was, as always, giving cause for concern. One of the major campaigners for improvement was Andrew Yarranton. In 1677 he enthused over the idea of linking the Severn with the Thames, first thought of ten years before, and gave his reasons for an inland route to the west coast. "Of necessity, we must always be sailing round about the Island, carrying and recarrying such heavy commodities from port to port to be taken into the most inward parts of the Kingdom, otherwise the charge of carrying such goods by land would rise to a very vast charge, the highways of our island being very uneven, and the ways therein in wintertime very bad".

Land carriage from London to Oxford at the time was about £3 per ton, three times more than by water, and the cost was very much greater when packhorses had to carry bulk goods such as coal or salt. Timber had to be left at the forest edge at the onset of winter rains and no attempt was made to haul it to the distant mill until dry weather returned, maybe six months later. There were of course delays on the river also but usually of only one or two weeks duration, although Yarranton states they could last six weeks.

Barges were still being held up by the contrariness of the millers and flashlock owners, especially during low water conditions, and exorbitant tolls were being charged. Complaints throughout the years led to the Act of 1695 when a new commission from riverside counties was formed and tolls and flash times fixed for a nine year period. Some of the details of the Act were as follows:-

"That a marke bee set above every lock within this County on this side the village of Bercott towards London at the charge of the tenant or occupyer of every such lock for the height to which the water ought to be penn'd above every lock for a flash if the water can bee raised so high, and that no tenant or occupyer of any lock or wear nor any bargemaster or bargeman do presume to remove the same.

"Certain justices appointed to view Hambledon lock and Marlow

Upper Thames Flashlock 1875

lock and sett the Flash Markes as above said and report to the adjourned session.

"The occupiers of all locks or bucks upon the River Isis or Thames on this side of the village of Bercott towards London shall keep their bucks and buckgates close shutt at all tymes, except as provided below, and except when the water in its constant course bee higher than the markes sett for a flash as aforesaid onely liable to bee drawn for the passage of boates downewards and upwards, which shall bee done in manner and forme following,

"The lock-keepers after notice given by the master or chiefe boatman of any boat — that any boat or boates are going down the river

104

from Cleeve with a flash shall draw their locks, etc., until the boats come to their locks or loose their Flash, of which the master or chiefe boatman of the first boat so looseing the flash shall forthwith give notice to the said lock.

"That no lock-keeper shall draw his lock upon any pretence whatsoever after the boats coming down with a flash have reached the lock next above his and notice of this has been given by the master of the first boat, except as provided below.

"When any boat has come down to a lock with a flash, as provided above, and the water is up to the flash mark, or so near as the lowness of the water permitt, and the bargemaster has ordered the lock to be drawn, then unless it bee upon a Sunday, the lock-keeper shall draw his lock and allow it to lye open for three hours, between Lady Day and Michaelmas, and for two hours, between Michaelmas and Lady Day, after the boats have shot the lock and for no longer, unless every of the said downward boates shall happen to loose their flash before they come to the next lock, in which case the lock-keeper concerned, the keepers of every other lock between that and the village of Bercott, shall immediately shut their locks for another flash.

"When the water is so low that it cannot be penned up to the mark and a boat has come down to a lock, then the occupier of every lock or mills shall shutt his mills for the space of three houres before the flash bee drawn unless the water rises to the mark in less than three houres.

"A boat and sufficient tackle shall be kept at every lock, and a winch in good repair which shall be made use of by every boat in his passage as hath been accustomed.

"In the case of boates coming up stream, the lock-keeper shall draw his lock as soon as required, excepting Sundays, unless he has had notice of a flash coming down. When locks are drawn in dark nights between the first of November and the first of March for any upward bound boat, the lock-keeper's servant shall be paid 6d. for one boat, and 1s if there are more boats, to be paid equally by the boats coming up.

"The lock-keepers shall keep their locks, etc. in good repair, and shall do all necessary repairs with such convenient speed and in such manner as may bee least predudiciall to the navigation.

"That the bargemasters or their servants shall give due notice of their boates coming down with a flash to all lock-keepers, and notice to the next lock of the boates loosing their flash.

"That every bargemaster shall keep his turn in shooting all locks and shall not attempt to gett one before another at the head of any

105

lock nor run on ground at any shallow place when the first boat is on ground to gett turne.

"That noe downward boat shall draw any locks or bucks before all the boates that give notice of the flash shall come to the lock, unless notice bee given of their looseing their flash as aforesaid.

"That whatsoever boates shall lose their flash shall light out of the way within three dayes after the flash is lost.

"That no upward boat shall attempt to wind any lock before any downward boat shall shoot it, if they happen to meet at a lock.

"The lock charges for all "locks, bucks and winches on this side of the village of Bercott towards London shall be as follows:- For Hambledon lock, 3s. 6d. all the year round, wether there bee occasion for a flash or not. Similarly for Marlow lock, 3s. all the year round."

The justices appointed under to put the flash marks on Hambledon and Marlow locks intended to meet on the 5th August to perform this duty. But owing to a misunderstanding, Stephen and James Chase, Edmund Waller and Henry Gould went to Marlow lock, whereas Sir Dennis Hampson and Johnshall Crosse went to Hambledon lock. The four justices at Marlow set "two spikes of iron, the one fixed by our direction in the first post of the Campshed on the northeast side of Marlow Bridge and the other fixed in a pile of the said bridge in levell as wee conceive to the last mentioned spike or at least to the lowest of the said spikes". They then went on to Hambledon arriving there at 6 o'clock in the evening. Sir Dennis Hampson had been at Hambledon since 11 a.m. with Johnshall Crosse, and his messages to the other justices had gone astray. While waiting, Sir Dennis "took a levell with a white willow stick and took the true heighth of the water to the campshed, sufficient to make a flash to carry off any barge and with a little detriment to the wears and locks. And if the mark had been sett one inch higher not withstanding 'twas insisted upon to have it 12 inches it would have been great damage to the adjacent meadows and to the said mills and wears". When they arrived, Mr. Waller and Mr. James Chase both disagreed with this point of view, and "Mr. Chase urged that it might bee placed by his direction alone or hee would not agree to anything. And (he) took the hammer and knock'd up the spike which the said Sir Dennis Hampson and Mr. Cross had fixed, and then attempted to drive a spike himself, which Mr. Cross knock'd off". Eventually, "night pressing upon them (they) parted without any further proceeding as to Hambledon Lock".

On receiving this report, the court confirmed the flash marks at Marlow lock and ordered the same justices, with the exception of Sir

Dennis Hampson, to settle the marks at Hambledon. This they did on 8th August, then they "sett a flash mark, by driveing a spike of iron onto one of the piles of the campshed of the winch, above a spike formerly driven by the said Sir Dennis Hampson". This mark was confirmed at an adjourned session held at Great Marlow on 27th August "at the house of the Widow Pomfrett, called or known by the name or sign of the Three Tunns".

6 · NAVIGATION IN THE 18th CENTURY

Early in the 18th century there were increasing tolls which were probably partly due to the increase in the size and burden of barges. Charges were also made for the use of towing paths, as horses were sometimes used instead of gangs of men. Strings of up to a dozen horses could cause considerable damage to towpath and river-bank, necessitating expensive repairs.

The Bucks Sessions records give a few more details of river traffic, particularly the carriage of malt. Before a local maltster could send his produce to the London markets the load was weighed and checked by the local excise officer and a duty paid. If by any chance the barge was sunk then the duty could be reclaimed through the courts. For instance, in 1705 the *Kings Arms* of Henley went down near Boveney and duty on 120 quarters was returned to five different Maltsters. (Defoe reckons there are about ten quarters to the ton). The following year *The Ship of Henley* also went down at Boveney, with the loss of 134 quarters, and in the same year *Little Dove* of Oxford, at Harlesford House above Marlow, with 165 quarters.

In 1711 *The Angell* of Henley sank at Marlow, and sixteen Henley maltsters lost 340 quarters, collectively receiving a rebate of over £80. A certain widow, Elizabeth Tovey, received £12 for 60 quarters. In 1713, the *Unicorn* of 90 tons burden left Hedsor Wharf with a cargo which included 32 quarters belonging to Beaconsfield maltster, Francis Carter. Only two miles downstream the laden barge went out of control at the great flashweir at Boulters, leaving another unhappy maltster up on the hill. Three years later *The Rose and Crown* was another Henley barge to go down at Marlow, laden with 410 quarters for London. Twelve Henley maltsters including Samson and Caleb, of the Tovey family, received the bad news and their refunds.

In 1723 William Davenport of West Wycombe and Thomas Darling of Great Marlow claimed that 57 quarters of malt on which they paid duty of £11 8s. had been sunk. It was afterwards salvaged and mixed with other malt, presumably after most of the surplus river water had been squeezed out. The two gentlemen received an allowance of £3 3s. as the local inspector reported that only part of the malt had been completely lost. In 1727 the total amount of duty on 105 quarters of malt (3s. 6d. per quarter) was refunded to Thomas Olyffe, Chiltern maltster, when the barge "Mealcock" went down at Boulters loaded with malt and paper. In the years 1732-9 Olyffe was sending 1,500 quarters to London annually.

Most of the foregoing claims were made at the Easter Sessions, which probably means that bargemasters were attempting to navigate during dangerous winter or early spring flood conditions and paid the penalty. With little or no insurance in those days the penalty was high. However, most cargoes got through reasonably intact, including in 1711 the Wycombe Parish Church Bells via Spade Oak Wharf to London where they were going for recasting, presumably returning the same way. An old brick farmhouse which may once have been part of Spade Oak Wharf still stands on the river bank just above the sailing club at Bourne End. The towpath from Cookham crossed the river at this point and continued to Marlow on the Buckinghamshire shore. At one time this was an important stopping place for the river traffic for in the middle ages the abbess of the nearby Nunnery of Little Marlow undoubtedly exacted a toll from bargemen towing through the estate which ran down to the riverside. The Nuns would have run a wharf on a commercial basis, receiving goods from London and exporting timber and country produce collected from the surrounding parishes.

After the dissolution the wharf continued to prosper and by the end of the 17th century was shipping out large quantities of malt. The Wharfinger then was Ralph Rose who was born in 1664 and who by 1701, either by inheritance or business acumen was rich enough to build himself a magnificent brick house in the nearby hamlet of Well End, where it stands to this day proudly bearing a terra cotta plaque with the initials R.R.1701 high up on an external wall. Ralph Rose is mentioned in the Buckinghamshire Quarter Sessions records in 1724 as Wharfinger at Little Marlow. Spade Oak Wharf and the nearby site of the old Nunnery are of course within the old parish boundary of Little Marlow but some way from the village which was sited away from the river on slightly higher ground. Ralph Rose lived to the ripe old age of 87. In 1751 he was buried in Little Marlow Churchyard where his grave may be seen today.

The importance of river traffic in the 18th century must not be under-estimated. It has been said that at one time up to 95% of goods

Lord Desborough inspecting the Maidenhead Floods 1894

to and from Reading were carried by water. According to Daniel Defoe the town of Reading was "A very large and wealthy town, handsomely built, the inhabitants rich and driving a very great trade. The town lies on the River Kennet, but so near the Thames, that the largest barges which they use may come up to the town bridge, and there they have wharfs to load, and unload them. Their chief trade is by this water navigation to and from London, though they have necessarily a great trade into the country, for the consumption of the goods which they bring by their barges from London, and particularly coals, salt, grocery wares, tobacco, oyls, and all heavy goods. They send from hence to London by these barges very great quantities of malt and meal, and these are the two principal articles of their loadings, of which, so large are those barges, that some of them, as I was told, bring a thousand, or twelve hundred quarters of malt at a time, which, according to the ordinary computation of tonnage in the freight of other vessels, is from a hundred, to a hundred and twenty ton, dead weight. They also send very great quantities of timber from Reading; for Berkshire being a very well wooded county, and the River Thames a convenient conveyance for the timber. They send most of it, and especially the largest and fairest of the timber, to London, which is generally bought by the shipwrights to the river, for the building of merchant ships; as also, the like trade of timber is at Henley, another town on the Thames, and at Maidenhead."

In 1723, one year before the publication of Defoe's *Tour* in which he extolled the wonders of Reading, the Kennet Navigation Company flattened the remains of the old castle at Newbury and proceeded to dig a huge basin and wharf capable of dealing with ten 100 ton barges at a time. The Act for 'The clearing of a passage for boats, lighters etc., upon the Kennet from the wharf or present common landing place at Reading to Newbury' was passed in 1714, but the work of building eleven miles of new cuts and twenty locks was not begun until 1719.

From the beginning the work was fraught with hazards, the greatest of which was the opposition of the Mayor, the Corporation and practically every man, woman and child of Reading. Up to that time Reading had the monopoly of trade over a vast area to the south and west. Much of this would now be lost to their lesser neighbour 16 miles away, so until the final completion of the scheme and the stabilization of management and tolls in 1730, the people of Reading did everything in their power to interfere with the construction work and tried to stop all early traffic. On several recorded occasions mobs of 300 or more, led by the Mayor, marched out to do battle with the engineers, breaking down new locks and sinking barges. Loaded barges were laid aground when the water was deliberately run off by sluicegates being left open, and when they finally reached Reading the crews had to run the gauntlet of the stone-throwing mob. In 1725 Peter Darvill, a Maidenhead Bargemaster, received a threatening letter which he brought to the attention of the authorities. It shows that river trade was so important that men would threaten murder to protect their livelihood.

"Mr Darvall wee Bargemen of Redding, thought to aquint you before tis too late Darn you if y work a bote any more to Newbury wee will kill you if ever you come any more this way wee was very near shooting you last time wee went with to pistolls and was not too minutes too late the first time your bote lays at Redding loaded Darn you wee will bore hols in her and sink her so don't come to starve our Fammeleys and our masters for Darn you if you do we will send you short home fer you have no aceation to come to teak the bred out of oure childrens mouths wee made an attempt wen your boat lay at bleaks bridg only your men must beene all drowned so teake warning before tis too late, for Darn you for ever if you come we will do it. From wee bargemen".

This letter is quoted by T.S. Willan in his useful article on the navigation of the Thames and Kennet in volume 40 of the Berkshire Archaeological Journal.

Despite all the opposition, Newbury became one of the greatest inland ports in the south. In company with other improved rivers and early canals, the Kennet set an example which led to the canal mania of the new industrial age.

The Thames-side towns were still growing in importance as more and more country produce was sent to feed the growing population of London. Thousands of tons of cheese and other goods were delivered yearly. In return London was sending up sea-coal to the amount of 80,000 tons a year. Many of the 300 or more barges now trading carried loads well in excess of 100 tons and when the stream ran fast between 30 and 60 men, or a dozen horses, might be required to haul them against the current. Thacker quotes a timetable of 1746 by Roger Griffiths, a City Bailiff, who lists barge departures from London for many local riverside towns including Guildford, two or three times every week, and also "to Abindon, Newbery and Reading from the Bull by Brooks Wharf, Queenhithe" every week, also a regular service to Oxfordshire.

Moulsford Timber Wharf 1897

Flashlock and Bridge tolls could amount to £14 for 60 tons to or from Lechlade to London. It is interesting to see that craft of this size could apparently negotiate the acute bends and shallow reaches for miles above Oxford without difficulty. High tolls were being paid at the three old pound locks and one other now at Sutton Courteney, where the miller was charging 35/- per passage. Down river, the Marlow toll was 4/-, a reasonable figure that was apparently to remain fairly static for the next fifty years.

In the mid-18th century the country began to stir out of its slow medieval agrarian existence. The country elite decided that there was money to be made from the new mines and machinery and in the mass-production of cheap goods to meet the needs of a growing population at home and abroad. The enclosures began to drive a new species of landless and lordless peasant into the crowded suburbs of the manufacturing towns where he was eager to subserviate himself to the mill owners, so that he and his family could live.

Many Acts of Parliament at this time centred on the attempts to improve transport facilities for the carriage of bulk raw materials and manufactured goods. The Death Penalty was imposed for stealing from barges and wharfs and on deliberate destruction of locks and weirs. The death sentence was also imposed on rioters who damaged the bridges and gates of the new turnpike roads, roads which might take a coach from London to Bath in two days, but which certainly couldn't cope with the many heavy stage wagons on which were imposed heavy restriction on weight and wheel size.

In 1729 came the first Thames Commissioners Act which was meant to obtain some control over the operation of flashlocks and the tolls charged "For the use of all towing paths, either by men or horses, as they are now used". The Act of 1751 appointed a new body to improve conditions on the Thames above Staines. Over 500 commissioners from the riverside towns, the University of Oxford, and gentry with certain property qualifications were appointed. Apart from annoying the bargemen with an unrealistic draught restriction of three feet (which was soon changed to four) and a temporary adjustment of tolls, things went on as they always had. By 1767 barges had reached the incredible load capacity of 200 tons. Flashlock owners blamed their increased tolls on the increase in the size of the vessels which in turn necessitated an increase in the heights of the weirs to give greater depth of water.

The first Pound Lock at Marlow in 1816

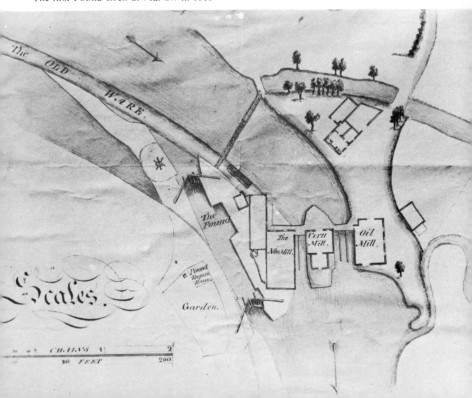

Old Windsor Lock 1865

In 1770 the Commissioners were reinforced by the addition of hundreds of minor landowners and town and parish officials and were soon to be jolted out of their complacency by several workable schemes for canals from Reading to London, by-passing the Thames altogether. James Brindley was commissioned by the City of London to survey the river between Maidenhead and London and to suggest improvements. He reported that twelve pound locks should be built (they were, about forty years later) but proposed that a better economic proposition would be to build a canal from Sonning to Isleworth, crossing the Thames at Monkey Island, Bray. The idea was enthusiastically received by Reading and the City but the Bill was voted out by Parliament owing to the opposition of the conveniently enlarged Thames Commission, which now included in its ranks most of the M.P's residing in the Valley. Several other similar canals, including one up the Wye Valley to High Wycombe, were proposed in later years but met the same fate.

The canal schemes did, however, frighten the Commissioners into getting on with the job of improving the river within their jurisdiction and inside three years turf-sided turnpikes, as they were first called — said to have been designed by Humphrey Gainsborough, brother of the painter — were built on the middle river at Boulters (on the Taplow Mill Stream), Marlow, Temple, Hurley, Hambleden, Marsh, Shiplake and Sonning. In fact, in all the positions in which locks exist today, except for the absence of Cookham which came sixty years later. Many other locks were soon to be built above Reading after pressure from the committees of the Thames and Severn Canal and the Oxford Canal which opened in 1789 and 1790 respectively.

In 1774 Bowles *Draught of the Thames* gave a total figure of £13 5s. 0d. in a table of tolls from London to Lechlade, including 7s. 6d. for the lock at Boulters, 4s. for Marlow Turnpike, lock, bridge and winch and 3s. for Temple Mills Lock and turnpike. In 1791 a 60 ton barge paid £26 16s. 6d. in tolls between Lechlade and London, almost double that of 17 years before. This was partly due to charges

Rebuilding the wooden lock at Mapledurham 1865

at the new pound locks (soon to decrease after yet more pressure from the canals) and also because tolls were still being claimed by the old flashlocks which the Commissioners were only just beginning to buy up. Freight charges were now about £1 per ton downstream and £1 5s. 0d. upstream between London and Lechlade and soon the Thames and Severn Canal company could offer rates of £1 6s. 0d. per ton for bulk cargoes all the way to Bristol.

A new Act of 1795 was supposed to reinforce the existing powers of the Commissioners and at the same time recommended that two pound locks should be erected in the Windsor area, at Cuckoo Weir below Boveney and at Romney Island, to help the navigation below Boulters. Permission had to be sought from the City of London in case obstructions such as these were likely to interfere with navigation below Staines. Of the two proposed, only the one at Romney was built. The Act also gave powers to widen and consolidate the old 'haling ways' for the use of horses.

At this time negotiations were taking place between the Commissioners and Frederick, Lord Boston, riparian owner of the dangerous Hedsor bend just below Cookham Ferry, where ferocious currents and rocky shallows had accounted for the sinking of a number of barges. It was considered to be one of the worst hazards between Reading and Boulters. Lord Boston was asked to clear the shoals and generally improve things, but made no effort to do so.

Towards the turn of the century the increasing canal trade boosted annual Thames tonnage through Staines towards the 85,000 mark, 70,000 tons passing through Boulters. The scene on the Lower River was that as described by an observer at Brentford ". . . vast numbers of barges coming up the river; they had wind and tide but they had all men to draw them up. I saw 34 men to draw up one but there was several more tied to him". Canals now brought many products direct from the Midlands and West Country to the Thames Valley, where in Reading groceries were as cheap as in London.

The famous Temple Copper Mills existed because of the Thames and Severn Canal. Smelted copper was brought from Swansea by Severn trows to the inland port of Brimscombe in the Stroud Valley, where it was transferred to canal barges for the rest of the voyage through England. Items of a more luxurious nature were coming through from the West Indies via West Country ports and bargemen enjoyed a lucrative sideline in smuggling, or alternatively suffered at the hands of gangs of raiders who plundered valuable cargoes of tea and sugar before vanishing into the remote Cotswold Hills.

7 · NAVIGATION IN THE 19th CENTURY

The first half of the 19th century saw the glorious peak of barge traffic on English rivers and canals. Soon the livelihoods of many water folk were to be swept away before the onslaught of the Railway Age. Had the canals been twice as wide and the locking system more efficient perhaps the commercial use of waterways would still be almost as important as on the Continent.

At the beginning of the 19th century the amount of essential goods carried on the Thames' network to and from the swarming Metropolis and Southern England averaged 84,000 tons per year, or the equivalent of over 800 barge passages. Total annual cargoes included between 2,000 and 3,000 cheeses from Buscot wharf alone and 20,000 sacks of flour from Reading. From Reading a single barge might carry 1,200 quarters of malt or other goods to the value of £2,000. Hay, wool and cereals, beech in timber and plank, billet wood used as fuel by the London bakers and hoops and brooms from the hazel copses of the Kennet, kept the country wharfs busy with the downward trade. To the valley came roadstone for the new turnpike roads and pottery and hardware from the Midlands down the narrow Oxford Canal, which also brought thousands of tons of coal from the Staffordshire collieries. More coal came from Shropshire and Wales via the Thames and Severn. Canal coal was prevented by statute from going below Reading because its price competed too well with sea coal from the London docks. Coal could still only be afforded by the more affluent members of English society. The poor still used turf, furze and brushwood for fuel. With the advent of gas lighting, yet further amounts of coal were required for gasworks in riverside towns. Other upward freight included ashes and rags for manure. The paper mills also needed vast quantities of rags as raw material.

Perishable articles were not often carried because of the fear of delays, although these were by now fairly infrequent. The flash system was still used twice a week during drought conditions, even at

Dutch Barge at Bisham 1834

the new pound locks. The Commissioners' bye-laws stated that all floodgates and sluices at locks and mills were to be drawn at Sonning on Wednesday at noon and then consecutively at each lock down river as the water built up to each "flashmark", reaching Boulters at one o'clock the following morning. Sluices had to be left open for three hours at each lock to allow upward moving craft to take advantage of the equalization of levels, after which the gates were shut to bring the water back to 'head'. The second flash was drawn at Sonning at 3 p.m. on Saturday, reaching Boulters at 4 a.m. on Sunday. In the winter flooding stopped traffic on less than twenty days a year. Occasionally there were greater delays such as the great frost of 1813-14 when Reading was deprived of all essential supplies for 12 weeks.

By 1809 there were twenty-six pound locks on the river, their dimensions being 110 ft. x 14 ft. from Oxford up to Lechlade, and from Oxford to Windsor 120 ft. x 18 ft. Some of the larger of the old Western barges were now being superseded by the 128 ton *Newbury* size of vessel that could use the important Kennet navigation with its

Spritsail Timber Barge 1853

LONDON and OXFORD

(BY RIVER THAMES).

THE LARGE AND COMMODIOUS NEW SALOON STEAMER, "THAMES,"

Leaves Kingston every MONDAY during the Summer Season, from about May 1st, to the end of Septem for Windsor, Reading, Oxford, &c., returning from Oxford for Kingston every Thursday.

TIMES.

KINGSTON BRIDGE,
Mondays, at 11·45.
(for Windsor).

WINDSOR BRIDGE,
Tuesdays, at 11.
(for Reading).

READING, (Caversham Bridge)
Wednesdays, at 10.
(for Oxford).

Returning from

OXFORD ., Thursday, at 10.
(for Henley).

HENLEY ., Fridays, at 10.

Arriving at Kingston same Evening.

FARES.

	Single
Kingston and Oxford	15
Kingston and Windsor	5
Windsor and Reading	7
Windsor and Cookham	1
Cookham and Henley	3
Henley and Reading	2
Reading and Oxford	7
Reading & Wallingford	4
Wallingford & Oxford	5
Oxford and Henley	10
Henley and Kingston	10
Minimum Fare, 1

The Steamer waits the arrival of the following

On Mondays, at Kingston, the 10.15 and 10.35 Waterloo, and 9.55 from Broad Street.

On Tuesdays, at Windsor, the 9.10 from Paddington and 9.30 from Waterloo.

On Wednesdays, at Reading, the 9.0 from Paddington and 9.0 from Oxford.

MARSH, BROS., PHOTOGRAPHERS, HENLEY-ON-THAMES.

Single Fare, 18/-; Return, 30/-; Intermediate, 3d. per mile.

REFRESHMENTS ON BOARD OF THE BEST QUALITY AT MODERATE PRICES.

Application for Hire of the "THAMES" on Saturdays, or for any day when not Advertised to run, to be made to the Secretary, at the Offices of the Company, Bath Street, Abingdon.

Full particulars may be had of

...ZE & SON, Tourist Agents, 113, Strand. | MARSH, Bros., Photographic Studio, Hart St., Henley | TOURIST COURT, Crystal Palace, Sydenham | S. COLLIER, Castle Hill, Windsor.
...ERRITT & SON, Royal Exchange. | J. SALTER & Co., Folly Bridge, Oxford. | GOLDER & Co. Market Place, Reading. | — JENKINS, Stationer, Wallingford.
...NGILL & Co., 371, Strand. | A. MOREAU, Queen's Road, Kingston. | — COOK, Stationer, Richmond. | At the Office of CALIGNANI'S *Messenger*, 10...

Or of the Secretary, at the Offices of the Company, Bath Street, Abingdon.

Announcing the first Upper Thames Steamer Service 1879

link to Bristol. In 1812 there were twenty-two Thames barges with Newbury masters. At the upper end of the river the Thames and Severn Company had twenty-five 70 ton Thames vessels as well as their other craft.

The Commissioners were entitled to charge 4d. per ton toll at their pound locks but the canal companies persuaded them to reduce this to 3d. to encourage business. Total tolls at the pound locks for the round trip to Lechlade and back came to 3s. 3½d. per ton, to which was added 1s. 9d. per ton toll at the 32 flashweirs still privately owned. Lock-keepers collected the tolls on the upward passage according to the registered tonnage. Half the toll was refunded if the barge returned empty, and a quarter if it was half full. So the Barge

122

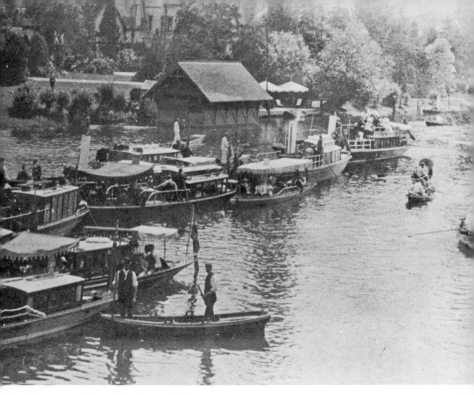

Steamers waiting at Boulters c. 1900

Master or Cost-bearer might have to find over £17 for tolls alone on the round trip, as well as a possible two week wage bill for a crew of up to six hands. Haulage fees for men or horses had to be paid and maybe a towpath toll was demanded by the riparian owners. The cost of haulage of a 128 ton barge could vary from 13s. 0d. per mile for 14 horses on the swift flowing tideway, to 3s. 6d. per mile on the Kennet. If we take an average of about 6s. 0d. per mile, which was the cost from Windsor to Reading, we have a total haulage cost over the 165 or so miles to Lechlade of about £50. This figure must be reduced to about £30 for the round trip as the Lechlade limit was a 70 ton barge, which required less pulling power than 128 tons, and only one horse was needed on the return trip. Sometimes the haulage cost would be negligible, for we must not forget that most vessels were equipped with sail which was used whenever possible.

The usual time taken from Lechlade downstream to London was

five days, from Oxford three and a half days, from Reading two days and from Maidenhead one and a quarter days. Thirty-five miles was a good day's, (and sometimes night's) run. This is not a bad figure when one considers that the modern Thames power cruiser takes about nine to ten hours for the same mileage, including locking time. The upstream journey took longer, twenty-five miles on a good day, depending on conditions. Lechlade was usually reached in eight days. The cost of carriage was now £2 per ton for the upward passage and £1 10s. 0d. down, about 2½d. per ton per mile. The cost of heavy goods by land, even on the improving turnpike roads was 1s. 0d. per ton per mile and could rise to as much as 2s. 6d. for valuable and perishable goods.

Between 1810 and 1815 there were further proposals for canals from the Kennet to Maidenhead and thence to Cowley on the Grand Junction Canal which was opened in 1805. At long last the City of London was stirred into constructing pound locks to improve the lower river. Six were built on the present sites from Teddington to Penton Hook. Bell Weir and Old Windsor came a few years later. By this time many of the up-river timber locks had been rebuilt or patched up on many occasions owing to the perishable materials

Hedsor Wharf c. 1820

Cookham Lock in 1865

used and damage by barges and floods. Gradually they were being replaced by more permanent structures. In 1825 Marlow received a new lock of Headington stone on the present site (to be rebuilt in 1927) and in 1829 a new cut and 'Ray Mill Pound' (only later to be called Boulters) was built at Maidenhead (rebuilt in 1912). The following year Cookham lock and cut were opened at last, by-passing the notorious Hedsor Bend.

With very few exceptions the Thames is deemed to be a public highway. Craft may navigate where there is enough water to float them as long as they obey the river laws. The major exception is the beautiful Hedsor Bend, now a backwater unknown to the majority of river users but which in the 18th and 19th centuries was spoken of rapturously by many travellers. One such was John Fisher Murray who in 1853 described the view from the Church.

"Few Parish churches are smaller than that of Hedsor, but few, very few, are so delightfully placed or so well worthy a visit, were it no more than to admire the delightful views afforded from the spot wherein it is situated. Hereabouts are many rotund knolly hills, of no very great elevation, yet commanding beautiful and extended prospects; some rejoicing in the richest verdue, covered with browsing flocks and herds; whence, sweetly softened by distance, comes across

125

the vale the tinkling sound of sheep bells: others coronetted with groves of venerable oaks, murmuring in hoarse and low sympathy with the freshening breeze of evening. . ."

Hedsor was conveniently situated on the main trade route out of Buckinghamshire and in consequence the lord of the manor reaped the benefits of his riverside lands, held under separate leases from the rest of the Manor.

The waters covered by the Manor extended from Compton's, otherwise Cobbs water, to Master Arthur Babham's. In 1556 there were two wharves, the main one leased to Thomas Godfrey and the other to Richard Over, a name perpetuated in Overs Farm in adjoining Wooburn Parish. In about 1570 Thomas Saunders took over "a wharf called New Wharf with a house thereon lately builded" to be called Saunders Wharf. The mellowed brick foundation of what is said to be this 16th-century building still stands near the Wharf House and this has recently been re-built into luxurious apartments. In 1579 both wharves were combined under one tenancy.

About this time the lord of the manor, Rowland Hynde, had a dispute with his neighbour, Henry Manfield of Cliveden, to whose family Henry VIII had granted Taplow and Amerden Manor as well as the Manor at Bullox, alias White Place, and other lands in Cookham. Manfield held Pages Wharf which must have served Cliveden House and nestled under the chalk cliff just downstream of the lower Hedsor boundary, and opposite Shawzies or Sashes Island. Hynde complained that Manfield had cut down willows on Shawzies bank which technically was and still is in Hedsor Manor, "whereby he might draw up by barge by Hyndes Water, which with his horses he did attempt to do two times in March last but did not prevail, as by affidavit appeareth". In other words this was an energetic attempt by a neighbour to take over the towing around the Hedsor Bend, which seems to prove that it was already an important source of revenue. This is the first reference to horse towing on the Thames. Subsequently Manfield attempted to divert the main current from the Hedsor Bend into his own Shawzies Water (part of which made the present Lock-Cut) by removing the ancient Warbor or artificial bank or fish weir at the head of Shawzies.

In 1594 one of the Over family held Hawkes Barn above Hedsor Village, which traditionally seems to be where the barge horses were kept. In 1605 Rowlands Hynde settled the estate on his descendants including "the wharves, horseing of barges and fishing in the river of Thames, with rights thereto belonging". Twenty years later the tenant was Richard Kynge. About 1700 Henry Turner is named as wharfinger and in 1717 Matthias Coldicott held both wharves with the privilege of towing barges. In 1734 Lord of the Manor Godfrey Parker leased the wharves to William Poulton for 21 years at £20 per annum and "one couple of good capons of the value three shillings, and in default three shillings in money and one dish of good and fresh fish of the value of three shillings on the first of May". Poulton was required to "make and drive one sufficient head pile at the upper end of the 'Warbor' above the bucks" and to "cast and scower all the flags, weeds, gravel, boughs, trees or any such stuff as shall gather ground upon Shawies," and to "plant the eyots". In 1764 the Irby family bought the estate and William Lord Boston became lord of the manor. According to Thacker local towing charges in 1770 for a 200 ton barge were:-

	£	s.	d.
Amerden bank to Boulters,			
7 Horses		12.	0.
Carter		2.	0.
Boulters Flash Lock		11.	6.
Boulters to Hedsor, 12 men at 2/-	1	4.	0.
At Turners Wharf, to Mr Wildmans,			
6 horses		8.	6.
Carter		1.	6.
At Spade Oak, to Marlow Bucks,			
8 horses		13.	6.
Carter	1	1.	6.
Up Marlow Bucks and Locks, 8 men		4.	0.
Marlow Lock		11.	6.

Prior to 1772 the Hedsor towing rights extended to Wildmans Mill (demolished 1895) on the River Wye, where it joined the Thames at Bourne End, but then the upper section from Cookham Ferry was closed and the towing transferred to the Cookham bank. Thacker says a certain Jas. King was now engaged for a year at £20 to transfer the barge horses across to Dodsons Close, by the church. A notice at the Hedsor/Cliveden boundary stated: "No horse is suffered to tow boats or barges here, but such as belong to the tenant of Hedsor Wharf, who keeps a proper supply for the purpose".

The Thames Commissioners now gave Lord Boston the towpath rights from his lower boundary to My Lady Ferry. This forgotten path lies precariously beneath the chalk cliff on the top of which stands Cliveden House. The Commissioners had purchased the path

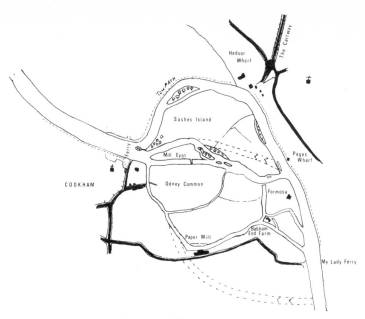

Survey map for Cookham Lock Cut 1808

from Lord Inchiquin in 1771 and widened it for horse towing. Lord Boston held this section until the opening of the lock in 1830. My Lady Ferry is said to be the site of a crossing of an ancient great west road, but there is no evidence to support this. The Ferry was opened in 1808 and passage was at first restricted to those concerned with the barge towing.

Over the years the Commissioners had received many complaints about the swift currents and shallows at Hedsor. Many barges had been sunk when they ran on to chalk rocks on the river bed. One such barge was the *Mary*, belonging to Jos. Gibbins of Abingdon. His tail of woe is quoted thus: "One of his barges was coming to London with Bath Stone for Westminster, and in the night of the 9th of August, the water being very low and the night dark; at Hedsor, she got aground and swung across the channel, which caused her to be broken in two. Loss about forty pounds". Despite incidents such as this, and official letters from the Commissioners, Lord Boston did little to improve conditions. In fact there was little he could do to increase the water levels which fell in the reach as Marlow weir was heightened, particularly around 1825.

In 1797 the Thames Commissioners' secretary Zachary Allnutt (who incidentally held Sheephouse Farm, Maidenhead, from the Powney family), approached Frederick Lord Boston regarding the purchase of the towpath, but was unsuccessful. When in 1802, the Wooburn and Hedsor meadows were enclosed, the Act held a proviso that the Enclosure Commissioners should not interfere with the towpath or the private road from the Wharf to Cookham Ferry (now a public footpath). In 1808, £500 was offered by the Thames Commissioners for the towpath and towing rights. Lord Boston replied that he would agree to this sum as long as the Commissioners excluded from public use, a short section in the grounds of the Wharf House which he claimed as exempt under the Act. As this was the central section of the path the Commissioners understandably broke off negotiations and began to survey for a new cut.

At this time the tenant was bound to "always be ready with two horses within one hour after notice given him" and if he were not ready, "The Barge Master shall be at liberty to draw up his barge with other horses belonging to him on payment of 6d. for each barge, as an acknowledgement to me, in right of my private towing path".

Up to 1829 the Commissioners were still trying to rent the path but at last lost patience. Alternative routes for a lock-cut had been surveyed in 1808, one across Formosa Island including part of the "Lollibrook" or Millstream, and the other across Sashes Island utilising part of the Sashes Stream. The latter route was chosen and the contract given to George Gyngell. The new lock and cut, costing about £130,000 was opened in October 1830. Nine weeks later, Lord Boston's tenant W.T. Hamaton, sold his horses and demanded and received remission of that year's rent of £73 10s. 0d.

So ended the commercial life of Hedsor Wharf. The steep, sunken cartway leading from the Chiltern heights no longer echoed to the shouts of the teamsters and the clashing of hooves. The fragrance of the shining stacks of Buckinghamshire beech no longer filled the air by the old wharf. Over 500 years of trade had come and gone, all that remained were a few stacks of coal which Lord Boston burnt in his private gas works up in the park. The average annual sum taken for the last three years of the Hedsor towing was about £590. The toll varied from 5/- to 25/- according to the size of the craft. In the last year, June 24th 1829 to June 24th 1830, 1555 craft of all kinds were horsed along the towpath.

In January 1833 Frederick's successor, George Lord Boston, wrote to the Commissioners demanding compensation. ". . . I feel myself aggrieved by the canal which you have cut, by which you have

Oil painting of Boulters Lock and Ray Mill 1842

diverted the navigation of the Thames and rendered my towing path on the banks of the Thames, in the Parishes of Hedsor and Taplow, useless to me". He demanded 25 years' rent, nearly £2,000, and £275 for his stables. At the Quarter Sessions he was awarded £1,000 plus £200 for the stables. Three years later the Commissioners appealed to the Court of the King's Bench but the earlier ruling was upheld.

For seven years the lock was operated without the help of a weir, Lord Boston refusing to allow any obstruction across the old Comptons Water, but at last the Commissioners got their way and erected a flash-weir on the present weir site below Cookham Ferry. Only Hedsor tenants were allowed to use it. Having been warned not to trespass on the sacred Hedsor ground, the engineers brought all materials to the spot in barges, drove in the piles to within two feet of the bank and filled in the gap with gravel thrown from the weir!

In 1843, after a long wrangle, the Commissioners agreed to erect a

Boulters Lock c. 1870

pound lock in place of the upper flash weir, with a new flash weir at the lower end of the estate incorporating an old stage of eel-bucks. It is believed that the pound lock was never used, except in 1845 by a certain Captain Hall who probably received a rough passage from the tenant. In 1869 the new Thames Conservancy reconstructed the upper weir as a fixed structure, thereby sealing off any through passage. Two years' later Lord Boston (now Florance) rebuilt the lower weir and eel-bucks, effectively sealing off the reach altogether, and so it has remained until the recent removals of the lower weir. A private notice now dominates the stream.

The Thames Preservation Act of 1884 states in its first clause that it "Shall be lawful for all persons whether for pleasure or profit, to go upon every part of the River Thames, through which Thames Water flows". But the second clause contained the proviso: "all channels which by agreement with the Conservators or Commissioners have been enjoyed as private channels for twenty years before this act shall be deemed not to be part of the said river". A further proviso read, "Provided that nothing in this act shall give any riparian owner any right against the public which he did not possess before this act, to exclude any person from entering upon or navigating any backwater, whether deemed to be part of the River Thames or not".

The Thames Conservators' 1894 bill was said by Lord Boston to prejudice his rights. He therefore petitioned the Parliamentary committee concerned, which later inserted a clause to the effect that nothing in the bill should take away any of the rights, privileges or titles of Lord Boston, or "other owner for the time being of the Hedsor Estate" in respect of Hedsor Water or the upper and lower weirs. Lord Boston later wrote, "The general result of the enquiry, whilst not giving the owner of Hedsor any expressed title to the water, undoubtedly strengthened his position".

When the Lock and Cut were opened the towing path was of course transferred to the cut side. Horse ferries were now required from Pages Wharf to Sashes Island and from the head of that Island to the Cookham village shore. When horse-drawn traffic ceased the Conservancy continued to operate the ferries for pedestrians until the 1950's when the cost of upkeep became too great for the negligible use made of them. Cookham Lock was rebuilt in 1908 and again in 1957, when electricially operated gates and sluices were installed.

The year 1830 was not only auspicious for the opening of Cookham Lock. This year the Wycombe Valley resounded to the clashes between workers and paper mill owners who had installed new rag grinding machinery and there were agricultural riots in Bucks. It was during this year that Brunel began to plan the Great Western Railway, which in a few years was to take away much of the water-borne trade of the Thames and its associated waterways. Despite opposition from many quarters, including the Thames Commissioners and the City of London, the G.W.R. Bill was passed in 1834. The line was opened to Maidenhead in June 1838 and two years later reached Reading.

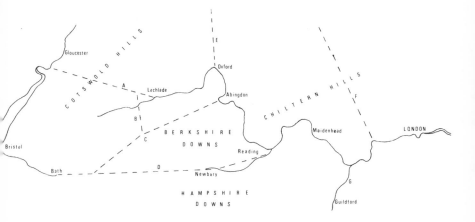

The River Thames and associated canals

There now began a fierce, but shortlived struggle for survival by many of the haulage firms dependent upon horses. Not only did stage coach proprietors urge their teams and drivers to make faster and faster journeys, but on rivers and canals in many parts of the country, light "Flyboats" carrying from 7 to 14 tons, surged on non-stop day and night services with goods and passengers. Three firms ran boats from London as far as Gloucester using double crews and relays of horses, but even these valiant efforts were exhausted by 1840.

Despite the railways however, the increasing population led to ever increasing transportation of raw materials and manufactured goods, resulting in continuing work for Thames barges, especially to those areas unaffected by the iron roads. Well into the second half of

133

Narrow boats on the Thames 1853

the 19th century the river still carried between one and two hundred barges a week. Many of these were narrow boats, but a good percentage consisted of the gracefully rounded successors to the vanishing square-ended Western barges. Up to the turn of the century and even later "Great barges with gaudily painted sterns were trailed against the stream by slow horses" on the through trade to Oxford, as well as supplying the local needs of farmers, millers and the rest of the riverside population.

The first canal to suffer from the attentions of the Great Western Railway was of course the Kennet and Avon. The Railway reached Newbury in 1847 and only five years later the canal was in a bad state of repair and the Company was forced to sell out to the Railway. Thereafter the traffic continued to decline, the railway company only doing vital repairs and allowing traffic where it suited them. In 1860 the once thriving Newbury Wharf handled less than 7,000 tons. In the first decade of the 20th century the figure had fallen to 3,000 tons, or about one pair of narrow boats a week. Thereafter most traffic ceased, although lock keeper, Edgar Light, recalls that as a boy at Sonning Lock during the 1914-18 war he saw forty foot long "sub chasers" working their way through to the Bristol Channel. By 1919 the sight of even a pleasure boat was so rare that Fred Thacker

134

Narrow boats under sail and towing 1853

caused "great wonderment" when he rowed up to Newbury. However, the Kennet and Avon Canal Trust is making valiant efforts to restore this beautiful waterway, although much money is still needed.

The Thames and Severn Canal underwent a similar fate. It had always suffered from water shortages and diminishing traffic returns, and debts left no money for expensive repairs. A canal which had seen nearly two thousand barges pass in a year, by 1890 saw but a few. The summit level lost water in 1895 and although in later years a few repairs allowed a trickle of craft through, the major restoration schemes came to naught and the canal was abandoned in 1927. Many of the old locks, and the impressive portals of Sapperton Tunnel lie as quietly crumbling monuments to the golden canal age.

Throughout the 19th and well into the 20th centuries, the canal network to the north of the Thames was vital to the rapidly growing industrial areas of the North and Midlands. Apart from the new railways, the main trading link with London and its docks was the Grand Junction Canal, which ever since its opening in 1805 had effectively short-circuited much of the traffic from the Oxford Canal.

Rebuilding Boulters Lock 1912

Replacing Boulters Tail Gates 1974

Even so, there continued to be a steady flow of narrow boats from Oxford on to the Thames. Horse-drawn 'worsers', lead boat and butty strapped side by side, sometimes with small square sails set, came silently down from their secret world of narrow waterways, the dark-skinned children wide-eyed at the stately Thames-side mansions and the glittering panorama of the London river.

The Act of 1857 gave the first Thames Conservancy body control of the lower river from Staines to the Estuary. For a while the old Thames Commissioners still held control of the upper river until in 1866 a new Act passed the running of the whole river from Cricklade to the sea into the hands of a newly augmented Conservancy. The old Commissioners were said to be "inconveniently numerous" and ill constituted; locks and weirs were in a very bad and dangerous condition and as tolls were greatly diminished there was insufficient income for repairs. Many workmen had to be laid off and officers worked at reduced salaries but even so £88,000 was owed.

In 1867 Thames Conservancy receipts from lock tolls totalled £2,550 from barge traffic and £1,020 from pleasure craft. Despite the advent at this time of iron steam paddle barges of up to 70 tons burden, the next twenty years showed a steady decline of commercial traffic tolls down to £1,174 in 1887, but pleasure tolls were steadily rising, in the same year reaching £3,805. This may show an increase in the total receipts but it hardly covered the cost of maintaining the river.

The new Conservators of the River Thames were given powers to eliminate many of the ancient practices which for so long had interfered with the proper control of navigation. The Act at last abolished the rights of millers to draw off water, relieved flashlock owners from the obligation to maintain their weirs and abolished the last of the absurd flashlock tolls. Other Acts followed, such as that of 1879, which allowed the Thames Conservancy to charge for water abstraction. The next administrative change came in 1908 when the Port of London Authority took over control of the river below Teddington. In 1974 there was yet another change when after more than a hundred years of river care the Thames Conservancy became a division of the new Thames Water Authority.

8 · BARGES AND BARGEMEN

The traditional clinker hull design and square sail of the Viking long-ship survived for centuries after other material remnants of that culture had been lost for ever. The basic design lived on in many types of coastal craft in various parts of Britain. Clinker hulls, tapering to a point at bow and stern could still be seen on the London river in the 18th century, although in many cases the square sail had given way to fore and aft rig more suitable for coastal work. On the other hand, the great Keels of the east coast rivers retained the square rigged sail up to the 20th century, but in this case the deep sturdy hulls became carvel built. On the west coast the graceful Severn Trow also became carvel built and developed a square-cut stern. The larger trows adopted fore and aft rig in the 18th century, but the smaller versions which negotiated the Thames and Severn Canal in many cases retained the square sail design.

Many different types of working barge evolved throughout the Middle Ages, the Humber and Newcastle Keels, the Trow, Billy Boy, Luff Barge, Hoy and eventually the famous Thames and Medway spritsail barges. They all traded from time to time on the River Thames, if only on the lower reaches. They all had two things in common, they were all built with reasonable freeboard to withstand a certain amount of rough water when sailing round the coast, and they were all flat-bottomed so that they could negotiate the shallowest inlets and rivers and could be beached to take on a cargo on any shore.

Similarly designed working craft from the Continent were a common sight in the Port of London throughout the centuries. Many traded far up-stream, catching or buying eels and lampreys which were used as sea fishing bait. Even in the 1930's Dutch eel boats called Schuyts were a common sight on the London river. There appears to have been a Dutch influence on Thames craft at a very early date for 'Shutes' are recorded as early as 1367, taking coal to Windsor and a 'Shoute' in 1414, taking stone down river to Westmin-

139

ster. Other early references to upper Thames craft are the 'ships' of the City of London in the 13th century, a lyghter laden with wine and other goods proceeding to Windsor in 1391 and barges taking goods to Henley in the 15th century.

At an early date simple rafts were undoubtedly used to ferry stock and fodder across from bank to bank and even carry heavy goods downstream, but these would have been too ungainly to have been used for general work. A working boat navigating solely on inland waters does not require a great amount of freeboard to withstand heavy seas. It must be stable, flat-bottomed for shallow waters, and of massive construction to withstand rough usage at the quayside and the inevitable battering from obstructions on the riverbed, as well as simple and cheap to build. All these requirements are fulfilled in the simple working punt of 'flat' which is still used for maintenance work and which has a history going back into the depths of time, not only on the Thames but on many working rivers in England and on the Continent.

The usual form of transport on the Thames in prehistoric times was undoubtedly the Celtic coracle, but from the Neolithic up to the Iron Age the dugout canoe was also a familiar sight. The remains of several have been found in the river-bed, such as at Bourne End railway bridge in 1871. Although the sides had perished it was evident that it had been carved from solid oak. The length was 25 ft. 3 ins. and the beam 3 ft. 4 ins., narrowing to an upward curving bow. The stern was square and there were two seats carved from the solid wood.

It is said that clinker-built craft evolved from the dugout and it could be that the punt shares the same ancestry. The basic punt consists of a flat keel-less base, with upward sloping square cut ends and parallel vertical sides, the whole being joined by knees and braces and carvel-built, that is, timbers butting up to one another rather than overlapping. The cheap box-like construction has its own built in rigidity and strength and no steaming of wood is required to fashion awkward curves.

We can assume that by the Saxon period punts were in day-to-day use for general carriage of goods between up river communities as their far greater stability and shallow draught would be preferable to the double-ended clinker boats of the coast. Increasing river trade throughout the medieval period brought a dramatic increase in the size of vessels and although the basic design remained, by the 16th century the punt had evolved into the once so familiar but now almost forgotten 'Western Barge'.

Tall master Western Barge 1793

The term 'Western Barge' goes back to at least 1548 and is probably far older in origin, so we can say that for at least 300 years they were a familiar sight on the whole of the navigable river from London Bridge westwards. Indeed they were such a familiar sight that in common with other everyday things of the past very little was written about them or their tough crews. Much of our information comes from more or less accidental pictorial representation by 18th- and 19th-century artists who sketched them in to fill up a space or create movement in sylvan scenes of hanging woods and stately riverside mansions.

Illustrations show that though their carrying capacity had increased enormously the Western Barges retained their primitive square cut hull design at least up to the end of the 18th century. In their heyday, barges trading from London as far as Reading reached a maximum length of about 128 ft., with a beam of 18 ft., and a maximum draught of 4 ft. when loaded and the amazing capacity of 200

141

Barge above Marlow Weir circa 1800

Relaxing at Oatlands 1822

tons, twice the capacity one can expect to find on most commercial inland waterways in England today. During the latter half of the 18th century, the largest barges were disused in favour of the 'Newbury' size which could navigate on the important Kennet Navigation. These were 109 ft. by 17 ft. and drew 3 ft. 10 ins. of water with a capacity of 128 tons.

In 1767 the largest barges capable of going further westwards to Wallingford were said to have dimensions of 128 ft. x 18 ft., carrying 170 tons, to Abingdon 112 ft. x 20 ft., carrying 135 tons, to Oxford 87 ft. x 17 ft., carrying 100 tons and to Lechlade 88 ft. x 12 ft. carrying 65 tons, all with a draught of 4 ft. Many of the barges were obviously too large to pass through the locks so must have continued to use the old flashweirs, which might be one factor which contributed towards their long survival. Westwards from Lechlade, barges of 6 to 7 tons burden went as far as Cricklade, where today it is unusual to see anything larger than a canoe.

Barges were built at many small slipways throughout the length of the river, in similar open situations as the barges of East Anglia depicted in John Constable's familiar painting. A typical Western

Barge had a flat-bottom made of 3 inch elm planks, possibly set transversely but more likely longitudinally, scarfed together and caulked. The oak sides were made up of longitudinal planks strengthened at the chine and joined to the bottom with knees and braces. Beneath the waterline the bottom probably curved upwards to the square outward slope or 'swimhead' of the bows and at the stern to the square-cut transom which was vertical and strengthened to take the massive wooden rudder. The upper edge of the hull was protected with a heavy gunwale. The inside bottom of the barge would have been strengthened and protected with floor planks.

The exterior of the hull was covered with black pitch but the sombre appearance was relieved by the brightly painted upper-works and the fancy lettering giving the owner's name, place of abode and the name of the vessel. Bargemasters took great pride in their vessels as can be seen by the names they gave them. Many were called after a favourite pub, such as *The Ship*, the *Rose and Crown*, the *Kings Arms,* and *The Angel*, all of Henley. Other names included *The Mary*, *True Briton, Unicorn, Little Dove* and *Mealcock*.

As with most craft using a single square sail the mast was set amidships. This position provided the sail with its maximum point of efficiency and also enabled the barge to be towed from the masthead without the bows being continually drawn in towards the shore. Barges were towed from the top of the mast rather than from a point lower down on the hull because of the great length and weight of the towline which had to be kept out of the water and clear of osier beds and other obstructions. Occasionally a line was taken from the bows to a point along the masthead towline to provide a lower pulling point. The mast was set in a tabernacle and could be raised and lowered in a matter of seconds by means of a line from the masthead leading to a great wooden winch in the bows. Other shrouds, three or four on either side and one on the stern, held the mast rigid under the strain of towing or sailing.

Throughout their voyages in all seasons of the year the crew's only shelter was a vast canvas awning on hooped poles, covered wagon style, occupying an area at the stern. Here they ate and slept in all weathers, their only heating probably some sort of protected brazier or clay-lined hearth, the beds nothing more than straw-covered benches. Apart from a small deck at the bows the remainder of the barge was completely devoted to cargo space. Heavy cargo such as coal would reach as high as the gunwale but lighter goods such as timber and hay were often stacked to a considerable height. Some barges even towed rafts of extra timber, and many had smaller lightening boats alongside, into which cargo could be transferred if shallow water was encountered.

The sail was used whenever wind conditions were favourable. It was possible to navigate downstream with wind assistance alone but more usual to have the assistance of at least one horse in difficult places. Going upstream, towing was the general rule, although the sail might be used as a supplementary source of power. The heavy towline was at least 220 yards in length and weighed six to seven hundredweight. As it cost about £10 and only lasted for about three voyages it was an expensive item.

Towing along Spade Oak Reach 1762

Strings of horses were already in regular use for towing from at least 1580 or so at Hedsor and presumably on other difficult reaches, but the use of horses and donkeys was the exception rather than the general rule until well into the 18th century. Until then it was usual to see gangs of ragged men waiting at town wharves and fighting for a chance to earn a penny towing up the next reach; barefoot, sometimes up to the waist in icy water, bearing on their shoulders a hand-tearing cable which in winter might weigh a ton or more when waterlogged or stiff with ice. Gangs of up to 80 men might be required during flood times but labour was easy to come by, there were always plenty of landless and destitute peasants, especially at the time of the enclosures. The Hauliers or 'Halers' as they were called, were "usually the worst possible character and a terror to the whole neighbourhood of the river", probably out of need rather than criminal intent.

145

On the other hand one gets the impression that the bargemen were thought to be a much higher class of person, well paid, and conscientious, and illustrious personages like Samuel Pepys, found them entertaining company.

The bargemen were notorious for their highly colourful and inventive language, "they use singular and even quite extraordinary terms, and generally very coarse and dirty ones, and I cannot explain them to you". They could also be violent. Pepys would have been well advised to steer clear of a certain William Honnor of Great Marlow who in 1682 pleaded guilty at the Bucks Quarter Sessions to stealing a saw, a case of knives, five pheasants, and other things from Sir John Borlase. Thereupon it was ordered that the gaoler "doe, upon Satturday next about the midd time of the day, fasten the said Honnor to the breech of a cart and strippe him naked from waste uppwards and whipp him from the gaole doore to the George signe post in Aylesbury and round the same, and soe to the gaole doore againe untill his body bee bloody, and soe to be discharged, payinge his fees".

Bill Honnor again came before the Court three years' later with three other Marlow men, for using guns, nets and "other engins" to

Spritsail barge at Bray 1865

"Millers Maid" of Hambleden 1880

destroy game, and again in 1690 with the Hubbart family, for unlawfully keeping nets for poaching. In 1694 he got Hugh Hydall, the Marlow constable, into trouble for allowing him to escape. In 1702, one would think old enough now to know better, he was indicted with Thomas Bray for rioting and assaulting John Bedient. In 1708, getting even more cantankerous in his old age, he and his wife were last heard of when indicted for being common night walkers, profane swearers and disturbers of the peace.

Bargemen were not above stealing from their fellows. In 1701 Jeremiah Hollis and Edward Lawrence were prosecuted by Marlow Bargemaster William Wast for stealing 20 yards of barge cable. However, they probably got a lot more fun out of cheating the more gullible of their earth-bound countrymen, such as in 1712 when two Oxford bargemen, William Rowland and his son, went on a jaunt to

147

Ballast barge leaving Bray Lock 1972

remote Winslow, in Bucks, and there defrauded linen draper William Giles and his son, "using and exercising unlawful games, i.e. cups and balls".

Despite their obvious shortcomings, the bargemen were a tough and fearless breed, and with the wherrymen of the lower river were a major source of recruits for the Navy. Many a young lad, after a rollicking night in the riverside pubs around Queenhithe, found himself impressed aboard a man o' war. Men were not even safe inland; in 1708 under an Act of Queen Anne, William Edwards and John Fryer were handed over by the local constables to Captain William Akers' Company in the Honourable Brigadier Hans Hamilton's Regiment "for the better and speedier manning of her Majesties' fleet." Many men jumped ship and some were recaptured back on their home ground. In about 1700 Daniel Holderness (a familiar surname in the area) a "Mariner belonging to His Majesties Ship The Sandwich" was ordered to be taken from Marlow to Chepping Wycombe Bridewell and detained until the Sherrif came for him.

A sailor's life was hard and uncertain with little pay, no pension, and if wounded, no insurance to fall back on. Only occasionally was £2 given out of County funds if the cripple could produce a certificate to prove he was wounded in action. The certificate that Benjamin Young showed the court stated that "he served his present Majestie in the late warr against the French by the space of four years in his Majesties ship called the Albermarle" and was wounded. A few years earlier in 1691, Marlow bargeman Ralph Thompson was paid £2 at the Wendover Sessions by one of the treasurers for the maimed soldiers, upon his producing a certificate that he "was imprest and sett on shipboard the Vanguard in the warrs against the Dutch in the year 1666, and the two fleets being engaged on St. James's Day in the same year and there was wounded in the right arme, shoulder, and cheek, and being now very impotent".

During the 18th century the greater part of the populations of riverside towns such as Henley and Marlow were said to be made up of bargemen, wharfingers and others connected with the river. They were a force to be reckoned with. After the disastrous summer of 1766 there were many riots over the price of food. At Marlow, bargemen took over the town and robbed the wealthier citizens, but instead of helping their starving women and children they went on a pub crawl to Maidenhead. Bargemen were again in trouble soon after the opening of the first Boulters Lock on the Taplow millstream in 1772. They found this a nice sheltered backwater in which to lay up and proceeded to use the grounds of Taplow Court as a thoroughfare into Maidenhead, making such a nuisance of themselves that a clause was inserted in the Act of 1774:-

"And whereas many trespasses have been committed in the Gardens and Plantations of Morough O'Brien Esquire of Taplow Court, by persons belonging to boates, barges, vessels, or floats, which anchor, moor, fasten, or lie, in Taplow millstream ... It shall not be lawful to anchor, moor, fasten, or lie ... in any part of Taplow millstream called Clemarsh Meadow".

The master of any vessel breaking the law could be fined up to £5. This law still stands, although it might to difficult to enforce today as a prosecutor would have to prove the position of the old lock, traces of which have long since vanished. Meanwhile the normal laws of trespass still apply and boats negotiating Taplow millstream are advised to keep moving.

Throughout the centuries pleasure traffic has received short shrift from the professional boatmen. An increase in the number of people using the river for recreational purposes is indicated in the Commissioners' bye-laws of 1804. There were complaints by "gentlemen and others, navigating on the river for pleasure, or otherwise", that they had suffered obstructions, threats and nuisances from bargemasters, costbearers and crews, who could be fined £10 for any such offence.

During the early 19th century there were many changes to be seen in the design of Thames barges. Sail patterns improved with fore and aft rig and spritsails became a common sight, later reaching perfection on the Thames and Medway spritsail barges. The opening of the Thames and Severn Canal brought the graceful Severn Trow hulls onto the Thames and builders were quick to copy the design. The "General View of the Agriculture of Berkshire" shows that as early as 1809 the rounded bows were common and also gives other information on the men and their working of a barge:-

"The construction of barges is almost universally the same, being flat-bottomed, with a rounded head; and as this form is as nearly capable of making speedy way through the water as any other, and as it does not prevent the barges being shoved sideways off the shoals, an inconvenience attending vessels whose heads are differently constructed, it does not appear that any improvement can be made in the shape of the largest barges. It is obvious however that vessels of this description do not easily obey the helm, and therefore the steersman is assisted by bargemen, who with large ashen poles, from 14 to 19 ft. in

Bringing a cargo from the Oxford Canal 1886

length, with incredible dexterity, keep the barge in the proper navigation channel. The occupation of a bargeman requiring not only
strength and activity, but considerable experience and local knowledge, is very lucrative. The number of persons requisite to work the
largest barges, is six men and one boy. One of the men, who has the
care of the vessel, and who defreys the tonnage, etc., is called cost-
bearer, or captain. With the stream downward, these barges require
only one horse, with which they travel after the rate of three or three
and a half miles in the hour; but against the stream in the upward passage, from 8 to 14 are necessary, according to circumstances". The
Act of 1828 relating to the laws and constitutions of Watermen and
Lightermen of the lower river, defined Western barges as all flat-bottomed boats and barges navigated from Kingston or any place beyond, and which were allowed to navigate down as far as London
Bridge. All vessels used for the carrying of passengers or merchandise had to have the name of the owner, place of abode and the name
of the craft painted on the stern in white capital letters and figures,
"the figures not to be less than six inches long, and broad in propor-
tion, and the letters not less than four inches long and broad in pro-
portion".

At the end of the 19th century the barges were still made of wood
and many were horse-drawn but the increasing use of faster steam
tugs required an improvement in hull design. The old square stern
gave way to the graceful 'D' shaped transom similar to that of the
Medway sailing barges, and latterly, the Wey barges. A cabin
beneath the stern-deck replaced the old hooped awning.

In this century the craftsman-built and gaily painted traditional
wooden barges have had to give way to their steel counterparts. Yet
even some of these retain a gracefulness of line which makes for easy
towing and causes scarcely a ripple despite a load perhaps in excess
of 100 tons of gravel dredged from the river-bed which is today about
their only cargo.

During the first half of this century there was a steady, though
declining flow of commercial traffic on the lower river mainly as far
as Kingston and Staines, the legendary Thames and Medway spritsail barges being gradually superseded by motorized coastal craft
and tugs and lighters. The Wey navigation continued to be one of the
most successful inland waterways in Southern England. As late as
1936 traffic could exceed a yearly total of 50,000 tons. William
Stevens' horse-drawn barges tied up for the last time in 1960.

In 1905 the river above Staines carried over 70,000 tons, much of it
going to and from the associated waterways such as the Wey and the

Diesel Tug "Pep" 1972

Oxford Canal but a considerable amount was made up of fairly local-
ised horse-drawn barge traffic on the higher reaches, such as the carriage of corn out of the Vale of the White Horse to Reading from
wharfs at Sutton Courteney and elsewhere. But already the mechanical age had disturbed the placid reaches of the upper river and by the
beginning of the century steam tugs were regularly used to tow timber barges up as far as Reading and occasionally to Oxford.

In the 1920's, Emmanuel Smith's steam barges, *Swan, Chinaman,
Laford* and *Boldsford*, transported timber, coal etc., towing six
barges below Teddington, four to Molesey, and three to Bray. A
maximum of two was allowed above Bray. At the same time, Mid-
land narrow boats from the Oxford Canal continued to supply coal
to riverside wharfs at Benson and elsewhere, and also brought down
mass-produced chinaware from Staffordshire and other goods from
the Midlands. Up to and during the Second World War, Odells' tugs
Leo, Rennie and *Oxford* were a common sight on the river as far as
Oxford. Raw materials such as rags for paper-making were brought
to Taplow, Temple and other mills and imported grain came to up-

153

T.W.A. Tugs "Cherwell" and "Churn" towing a maintenance barge in flood waters 1975

river corn mills at Marsh and Sonning. The trade continued to Sonning Mill until 1952, when after a series of lock closures it was found to be economical to use road haulage. One last short-lived attempt by a miller to use the river commercially was made in 1959, when chicken food was brought to Marsh Mill direct from London Docks by narrow boat in two days.

From the 1930's, Samuel Becketts' tugs, *Vim, Pep* and *Pygmy*, towed special Dutch-built iron swimhead barges on regular runs to the great timber yards at Kingston, Marlow, Reading and Oxford. Not only did the tugs have quite comfortable living accommodation for a week away from home but the long tradition of a semi-nomadic river life was also perpetuated on the great 100 ton barges, where cramped quarters were provided in the stern for a couple of bargemen or sometimes man and wife. The immaculate tugs, towing two brightly painted barges stacked high with imported soft woods must have made a brave show as they swept up river. Many planks disappeared overboard, giving rise to a rash of new riverside sheds and even bungalows. Sometimes a tank barge might be dropped off at Maidenhead gasworks wharf on the way up, filled with 'gas oil', and picked up a few days later as the tug left Boulters Lock on the way back to London.

During World War II Simmonds Brewery at Reading made a valuable contribution to the war effort by exporting beer to the troops overseas. A regular barge load of barrels would leave Reading en route for London Docks and weave its erratic way down river, miraculously steered by a bargeman nonchalantly leaning on the tiller because he was too drunk to stand up! Lucky was the lock-keeper who had the barge tied on his layby overnight.

The merchandise figures for the river above Teddington almost doubled during the war, reaching over 600,000 tons in 1944. The average of about 300,000 tons per annum was maintained into the 1950's, but thereafter came a dramatic fall to a miserable 4,000 tons in 1972.

* * *

As far as the future of the Thames is concerned, as long as there is not too much concreting of the river banks, not too many gaudy marinas, and some curtailment of suburban sprawl, with luck the wildlife will continue, and the river will remain beautiful for many generations to enjoy.

INDEX

A

Acheulian style hand-axe 20
Ashley Hill 18
Atrebates 28

B

Babham family 56
Barge Pole, the (Marlow) 45
Beaconsfield 20
Belgae 28
Bickersteth, Archdeacon 22
Bisham 24, 90
Black Park 19
Boulter's Lock, Maidenhead 16,
    52, 53, 108, 109, 117, 118, 125,
    149, 155
Bourne End 16, 27, 29, 79, 91, 109,
    140
Boveney 108
Boyne Hill 19, 20
Bray 15, 24, 28, 29, 32, 34, 35, 43
Braywick 24, 26, 31
Brindley, James 116
Brunel's railway bridge,
    Maidenhead 15, 46, 95, 133
Burcot 96
Burnham 20
Burial mounds 26

C

Caesar, Julius 28
Catuvellauni 28

Caversham 88
Chertsey 88
Chiltern Hills 18, 19
Clactonian tools 21
Clifton Hampden 21, 96
Cliveden 16, 21, 40, 41, 52, 62, 127
Cockmarsh 16, 30, 31, 32
Compleat Angler Hotel 17
Cookham 16, 18, 26, 27, 28, 29,
    30, 31, 32, 34, 35, 38, 48, 54, 56,
    57, 59, 62, 74, 88, 91-93
Cookham Dean 17, 46

D

Danesfield 27
Datchet Ferry 103
Domesday Survey 32-33, 66, 71
Dorney 40

F

Fisherman's Arms, the, Marlow
    45
Flackwell Heath 80
Flint tools 22
Formosa Island 38

G

Goring 19, 103
Goring Gap 19, 21

H

Hallstatt culture 26, 27
Hambleden 29, 115
Hampton 88
Hedsor 16, 20, 29, 37, 62, 76, 79,
118, 125, 126, 127, 128-130,
132
Henley 18, 20, 88
High Wycombe 31
Hurley 115

I

Iffley 96, 99

K

Kennet & Avon Canal 134, 136
Kennet, River 20, 22, 112, 113
Kingston 88

L

La Tene culture 27
Levallois flake tools 21
Little Marlow 17, 58, 76, 109
Loudwater 78
Lunnon family 76
Lynch Hill 19, 20

M

Maglemosians 22
Maidenhead 15, 16, 18, 20, 24, 27,
28, 30, 33, 45, 46, 53, 54, 58, 73,
81, 88, 89, 90, 92, 95
Marlow 15, 17, 20, 28, 29, 30, 45,
67, 79, 88, 89, 108, 115, 149
Marsh 117
Medmenham 27
Mesolithic period 24, 47

N

Neolithic settlement 24, 47
Newbury 112, 113

O

Odney 38, 62
Oxford 21, 96

P

Port of London Authority 138

Q

Quarry Woods 17

R

Reading 20, 112
Reinbald 32
Remenham 18
River Act (1695) 103
River Improvement Act (1624) 96
Rose, Ralph 109
Rowborough Hill 16, 17

S

Sandford 96, 99
Skindles Hotel, Maidenhead 16
Sonning 115
Spencers Farm, Maidenhead 33
Staines 88
Sutton Courteney 114
Swift Ditch 96, 99, 100

T

Taeppa's burial mound, Taplow
31
Taplow 16, 18, 19, 20, 21, 28, 29,
31, 40, 43, 59, 60, 74, 75
Taylor, John 100
Temple 66, 115, 118
Thames & Severn Canal 136
Thames Water Authority 138

W

Well End 109
White Place Farm 38, 39, 40, 41,
72, 126